DRIVING TO MY APPOINTMENT WITH DEATH

The Lessons Grief, Loss, and Love Taught Me About Living Fully

Venice Ishibashi

ISBN: 979-8-9931402-1-6 (Paperback)

ISBN: 979-8-9931402-0-9 (Hardcover)

ISBN: 979-8-9931402-2-3 (eBook)

Book design by Dara Publishing LLC

Place of Publication: Brooklyn, New York, 11226

Library of Congress: 2025919740

Printed in the United States of America.

Disclaimer: The publisher and the author do not make any guarantee or other promise as to any results that may be obtained from using the content of this book. This publication is meant as a source of valuable information for the reader. However, it is not a substitute for direct expert assistance. If such a level of assistance is required, the services of a competent professional should be sought.

DEDICATION

To Marvin, my little cousin.
You were just a kid. Full of light. Full of life.
Losing you so young broke something in me that never fully healed.

To Mama, my grandmother, my safe place.
You gave me love with no conditions and strength without words.
Even when your body grew tired, your spirit carried all of us.
I still feel you near me when I need it most.

And to every person I've watched fade because of cancer.
Family, friends, people I love, and people I barely got to know.
There's something cruel about watching life slip away so slowly,
but also something sacred in bearing witness to it.

It was in those moments standing at bedsides, sitting in silence,
asking questions for which no one had answers, I began to wonder:
What are we all living for?

This book was born out of that question,
and out of the pain, love, and longing you all left behind.

Thank you for being part of my story.
This is for you.
And for all of us searching for meaning in the midst of life and death.

This book reflects how I view life—not as a linear checklist,
but as a journey, full of detours, rest stops, laughter,
quiet stretches, and awe-inspiring views.

Life has constantly reminded me of a road trip.
We start somewhere, we end somewhere,
but what truly matters is how we travel in between.

I've experienced joy, heartbreak, transformation, and the unexpected.
All of which have shaped my journey.

I wrote this as a way to help you reflect on your own road,
with the hope that you'll find peace not just in your destination,
but in every twist and turn that gets you there.

Buckle up, it's time to ride.

TABLE OF CONTENTS

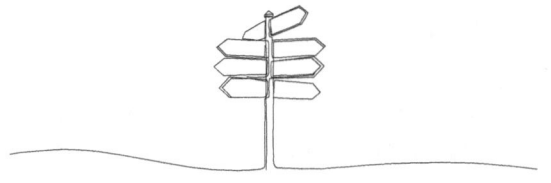

Introduction
Before We Drive

Why This Ride Matters

The first time I saw cancer up close, it was in my godsister Terry's eyes. She was in the last two weeks of her life, and I will never forget the fear—hers and mine. Cancer wasn't just something I heard about anymore. It became something I saw. It was the way her body changed every day. It was the silence in the room when there were no more words. Watching her suffer while cancer ripped her apart was terrifying.

She died on my birthday.

After that, I stopped celebrating for a few years. Not because I didn't value life, but because I no longer saw the sense in it. Her death made me feel like birthdays were not about getting older, but about getting closer to the end. Each one became a reminder that I was one day nearer to my own death.

That moment changed something in me. It forced me to start asking different questions.

What are we really living for?

What are we doing with the time we're given?

This book is not a self-help manual. It is not a list of instructions. It is a reflection.

It is how I see life, not as a straight line, but as a road trip. There are rest stops, wrong turns, beautiful views, breakdowns, and unexpected detours. We start somewhere. We end somewhere. But what matters most is how we travel in between.

I've lived through joy, heartbreak, confusion, loss, and growth. And through all of that, I've tried to make sense of what this ride is really about. Writing this book has helped me process my own journey, and I hope it helps you reflect on yours.

You don't have to be in crisis to read this. You just need to be honest about where you are and where you want to go. Because once you start asking the real questions, the road begins to feel different.

This book is for anyone who has sat in grief and tried to breathe. For anyone who looks at birthdays with a quiet ache. For anyone who has lost someone and felt the shift inside them that doesn't quite go away.

So, before we go any further, just know this: this ride matters. Not because of where it ends, but because of everything that happens along the way. And you deserve to be awake for the ride.

You might be wondering why you should take this trip with me or what you'll find along the way. Here's what I can tell you: this book will not promise you that the road will always be smooth. It will not tell you that pain is avoidable or that joy comes without effort. Instead, it will walk beside you as you navigate your own miles, offering moments to pause, reflect, and see your life in a new way.

Through these pages, I'll share parts of my own map, the moments I got lost, the unexpected detours that led to something better, the passengers who changed me, and the stretches of road that tested my faith. You'll see where I found beauty in the mess, where I learned to slow down, and where I discovered that every mile—even the hard ones—had meaning.

We'll travel through ten chapters, each one like a leg of a longer trip. You'll see themes of loss and love, struggle and resilience, fear and faith. You'll meet the people who rode beside me for a while and the ones I had to let go of. And you'll be invited to consider your own passengers, detours, breakdowns, and scenic views.

This is not my journey alone. It is an invitation for you to think about your own.

Along the way, I will ask you questions. Not the kind that require quick answers, but the kind that sit in the passenger seat and keep you company for miles.

I will not tell you how to drive. I will simply share what I have learned by being on the road, about noticing the view, about knowing when to pull over, about forgiving yourself for missing the exit, and about trusting that even the longest, hardest miles are still part of the trip.

Let's Begin

If you've ever been on a long drive, you know there's a moment when the engine hum becomes part of the background, and you forget you're moving until something catches your eye—a bend in the road, a flash of sunlight, a sign for a town you've never seen before.

Life is like that. We can get so used to the rhythm of going through our days that we stop noticing the small moments that make them worth living. This book is my way of pulling over with you for a moment, of looking at the map together, of asking if we're still heading where we want to go.

We will start where every journey begins: at the decision to leave the driveway. In the first chapter, I'll take you back to a time when I realized that if I wanted to live fully, I couldn't just sit behind the wheel with the engine running. I had to put the car in gear, even if I wasn't entirely sure where the road would take me.

There will be joy ahead. There will be loss. There will be detours we didn't plan for, and scenic routes we didn't know existed. But if we travel with open eyes and an open heart, there will also be meaning, and meaning is what makes the miles matter.

So buckle up. Roll the windows down if you like. The road is waiting, and the ride is ours.

CHAPTER

01

The Ignition

What We Inherit Before We Begin

We're passengers at first, completely dependent on others for everything: nourishment, love, protection, guidance. Our caregivers are the first drivers, navigating the road on our behalf while we sit strapped into the back seat, staring out the window in wonder. The world rushes past us: colors, sounds, faces. Even though we don't yet understand it, the car is moving and we are alive, experiencing the earliest stages of the ride.

Each new experience is like a road sign or a landmark. Our first steps, our first words, our first fears all are impressions taken in through the window of life. Though we cannot recall these early miles, they leave invisible marks on us. The way we're handled, the tone of voices around us, the consistency of care or chaos . . . it all shapes our interior. Our sense of safety, our attachment to the world, our basic trust—these are the early alignments of our vehicle's steering.

The road in these early years may feel smooth or rough, depending on who's behind the wheel. Some are born into loving homes with careful drivers, parents or guardians who communicate love clearly, who offer stability, who brake gently and steer with purpose. Their cars may not be flashy or new, but they're steady. The ride is filled with enough predictability to let a child exhale. But others are buckled into vehicles driven by people still learning how to steer, who navigate with a trembling hand and blurred vision, unsure of the destination or how to even get there. And then there are those whose drivers should never have been behind the wheel at all, those guided by addiction, rage, or unresolved trauma, or those who are absent entirely. For them, the road is a series of potholes, detours, and wrong turns. Still, the vehicle presses forward.

I know this road well. My mother was young, raising four kids and her younger brother, hands still shaking from her own childhood. Her love wasn't absent, but it was hidden behind exhaustion and silence. And as a child, I didn't always know how to read that silence. Was I being pushed away, or was I being ignored? That confusion followed me into adulthood. Some days, she was a warrior, a woman who held everything together with nothing but grit and a bag of peanuts. Other days, she seemed barely able to hold on. But she kept us moving.

I remember her pregnant with my little sister, working long hours at a factory. I had never seen it but my imagination created this place not built for comfort, just rows of tired women sewing bras for long hours in the heat and very bright light so that they did not make any mistakes. Most days my mom came home with swollen ankles and tired eyes. She wore borrowed maternity dresses until one day, after an argument, the woman who lent them took them back and humiliated her in public. My mother stood there, stripped of dignity, but she didn't break. She carried on. I didn't understand it then, but now I see: that was power. Quiet, consistent, often invisible power.

She was trying to steer a car she never learned to drive. There were days she looked lost, like life had handed her the keys without a map. And yet, despite the scarcity, the setbacks, and the sacrifices no one applauded, she kept us moving. Her willpower became our vehicle, even when the wheels were wobbly. My dad was always there but he struggled to keep a job and the first chance he got at a decently paying job, my mom encouraged him to buy us a home and so he did.

One memory of my childhood haunts me. I was around ten when I followed my family to the home of a man who had taken his own life. He had hanged himself in his yard on a bright, beautiful morning. The adults spoke about it with a chilling matter-of-factness, like it was something we were supposed to accept. But I couldn't. As I stood in the yard, looking at that young, strong man hanging from the tree with the sunset peeking through the branches, I felt outside of myself and confused, my young eyes struggling to comprehend what I had just been exposed to. The idea that someone could simply decide to stop being alive and a part of this world . . . that shook something loose inside of me.

I remember thinking: anyone can just decide to take their life. Just like that. It was the first time the fragility of life became real. I didn't feel safe after that. Not in the world, and not in my own mind. That moment planted a seed of quiet vigilance in me, one I still carry. I remember lying awake that night, staring at the ceiling. I kept asking myself: could I ever become that lost? Could someone I love? It wasn't just fear. It was the beginning of a deep, lifelong need to protect those I love from falling through the cracks. It taught me to pay attention, even when no one else seemed to. And that is the reason I don't really text my friends and family. I like to pick up the phone and call them to let them know that I am checking in on them.

Then there was the night a man from our community (known for his drinking) fell into a ditch and died on his walk home. I heard my family talking about it and so we all went to see him, which was the norm in the community. Lifeless. Alone. His body lay twisted and cold in that narrow ditch with a trickle of water running through the bushes in its path, and for the first time, I understood the full weight of what it means to leave this world unseen, unheard, unaccompanied. That night stayed with me. Not because I knew him well, but because it felt like death itself had walked into our neighborhood and quietly taken someone away. No noise, no drama, just gone. I couldn't close my eyes that night. I just stayed awake, restless. It wasn't just that he died, it was how he died. Alone. Without anyone to catch him, hold him, or notice he was slipping away. That truth settled into me like a hot stone from a spa: that people could vanish and the world would keep moving. It terrified me.

Up until then, I thought adults were invincible. I believed someone would always be there watching, helping, stopping the worst from happening. But seeing the man who died in the ditch shattered the illusion. That night, I learned that grown-ups could fall too. That they could be lost and broken and no one might even notice until it was too late. It made the world feel less safe. I began to wonder who else was quietly falling apart around me. I started watching more closely, listening more carefully, because if no one else would notice, maybe I could.

I think that was the beginning of my hyper-awareness, the quiet alarm inside me that never fully shuts off. A constant scanning of the people I love, the silences between words, the heaviness behind smiles. I didn't have the language for it then, but I was searching for signs. Signs that someone was drifting, signs that someone needed help, signs that someone didn't want to be here anymore.

Because I never wanted to feel that powerless again. I never wanted to be caught off guard by death slipping through the cracks of everyday life.

Years later, when my cousin Marvin died in his early twenties, that truth returned. Marvin knew he was going to die and he made peace with it. He wasn't angry or afraid. He moved through those final days with a calm that was both unsettling and inspiring. And I kept asking myself: how do you do that? How do you face death with peace when you've barely lived? Or maybe that was his full life. Maybe that's all he was given. Maybe the measure of a life isn't in the years but in the way we travel through them. Marvin smiled in the face of the inevitable. He taught me that peace isn't about how much time you get, it's about how you hold that time. He faced the end with a grace that made me reflect on my own fears, my own resistance to the unknown. In his stillness, there was wisdom. It was as if he had already visited that place we all fear and had come back to show us that we could carry light into the dark.

His peace eased my panic, yet I was angry that he was okay with death. It made me realize how much I was still afraid not just of death, but of living the wrong way. Watching Marvin surrender with such quiet strength forced me to look inward. What was I still holding onto? What was I afraid to let go of? I began to question if I was truly living, or simply surviving, checking boxes, avoiding pain, hoping that fulfillment would find me instead of seeking it out with intention.

His death didn't just make me mourn him. It made me examine myself. I saw how often I'd been driving on autopilot, letting fears and grief steer my direction. Marvin's grace in the face of God at the end became a mirror, showing me that peace isn't passive. It's something we build mile by mile, choice by choice. And I wanted that kind of peace. The kind that doesn't wait for the final breath to feel free.

We don't choose our beginning, our parents, our environment, our health. But we inherit a vehicle (our body, our mind) that will carry us through life. Tuning this vehicle matters. Understanding where the road began helps us decide how we want to travel next.

We inherit more than just eye color and blood type. We inherit beliefs, fears, dreams that weren't ours to begin with. We inherit coping mechanisms wrapped in silence, anger passed down like heirlooms, and resilience taught not through words, but through survival. Some of us are handed vehicles in mint condition, well-tuned, well-kept, ready for the ride. Others get cars that stall at every corner, engines that sputter and wheels misaligned from years of trauma. But regardless of the condition, this is the vehicle we begin with. And what we do with it, how we tune it, maintain it, and eventually, how we drive it—it's up to us.

Understanding where the road began allows us to give context to our patterns. Why do we react the way we do? Why do we fear the things we do? Why do we crave certain types of connection or avoid others altogether? Our early passengers, the voices that surrounded us, might still echo inside our heads. And sometimes, their directions still guide our choices.

But here's the truth: we can recalibrate. We can adjust the mirrors. We can replace the tires. We can learn to listen for the knocks in the engine and get help before we break down completely. We don't have to drive the way we were taught. We don't have to follow maps that lead nowhere. And we don't have to keep traveling roads that hurt us just because someone else paved them.

This chapter is a reminder that while we may not control the beginning of the ride, we can take the wheel when we're ready. We can decide how fast we go, when we stop, what routes we explore, and what we leave behind.

Our inheritance may explain our start, but it doesn't have to define our finish.

For me, that realization crept in with the birth of my two sons. Everything shifted. Suddenly, I wasn't just protecting my own life. I was responsible for theirs. I remember holding my firstborn son for the first time and thinking, *I have to teach him how to drive a road I've barely learned myself.* That changed how I saw the road. I started recognizing that my family's way of navigating life wasn't the only way and wasn't always the right way. I began creating my own path, one carved from the lessons they gave me and the ones I learned from pain.

There was a night my eldest was barely three when he threw a tantrum so fierce I could feel the frustration rising in my chest like a wave. I had no blueprint for this. My instinct was to yell, to shut him down, to silence the noise before it got too big. That's what I had known growing up. Silence and shutdown. But I caught myself. I saw his little face, red and trembling, and I realized he wasn't trying to defy me; he was trying to be understood. I sank to the floor beside him, pulled him into my arms, and whispered, "It's okay to feel. I've got you." Then he calmed down and I said to him, "I have never been a mom before, so I am going to need your help. So please understand that I am learning to be a mom from you." That moment wasn't perfect, but it was memorable. It was mine, and it was intentional, and the way he looked at me, we understood each other.

I remember thinking, *This is where the road splits. This is the turn I didn't get as a child.* In that quiet moment, I made a vow I would not raise my boys in fear of their own voices or emotions. I would show up, even when I didn't have all the answers. I would drive differently. That one small pause taught me that healing sometimes looks like stopping where our parents accelerated.

There have been countless times I've smiled with tears pressing behind my eyes, holding in feelings that had nowhere to go. I've learned that people often only see what you allow them to see and many times, what they care about is what you can do for them, not who you are beneath the surface. That's a hard truth to carry. To be needed and invisible at the same time. To be strong for others while trying to find strength for yourself.

And yet, I drive on. I've tasted success. I'm still chasing more. But I now believe it's not about winning the race, it's about finishing it. Every traveler has their own start time. Some journeys begin with a roar, others with a low rumble. What matters is that we keep moving.

I had a destination I couldn't yet name, but I knew death was somewhere down the road. And what I inherited would shape how I got there unless I learned to drive differently. Ignition wasn't just the beginning of life, it was the start of a journey I didn't know I was on.

Because it didn't start with our choices; it started with what we inherited. And knowing that helps us understand how we want to travel from here. We carry maps drawn by others, but we are not bound to their destinations. We can pull over. We can chart new directions. We can learn to read our own compass and write our own legend across the miles ahead. Even when we've been handed broken steering wheels or unreliable engines, we are not doomed to repeat the ride. We can repair it. We can rebuild. We can drive differently.

We are all traveling, and our destination awaits us. But while you're on your way, stop and tell someone that three miles back, there's a sinkhole. Warn them. Hug them. Hand them a map if you can. That's how we help each other arrive. That's how we travel with grace. That's how we turn survival into something sacred.

Because this isn't just a story about where I've been. It's about where I'm going and how I plan to get there with purpose, honesty, and heart. And if you're reading this, maybe some part of you is searching for that same grace. The kind that turns pain into wisdom. The kind that says, "You don't have to travel alone."

There was a time in my life when I was so focused on survival that I forgot what it meant to dream. I was moving, checking boxes, fulfilling obligations, making sure everyone around me was okay. But inside, I was tired. Disconnected. I had confused motion with meaning.

It wasn't until I paused, really paused, that I realized I was allowed to choose a different way. I remember sitting in my car one evening after a long day, engine off, hands still on the wheel. I didn't cry. I didn't speak. I just sat there, listening to the hum of silence and my own heartbeat. And in that stillness, I heard something I hadn't heard in a long time: myself. My real self. Not the version others needed or expected but the version that longed for peace, for joy, for something more than just making it through.

This book was born out of that moment and many like it. It's not a roadmap, but a mirror. A reflection of what happens when we slow down and ask ourselves where we're headed and—importantly—why we're headed there. And who we're becoming along the way.

So if you're still reading, my hand is stretched out across these pages. I want you to know you're not alone on this road. Maybe you've had your own breakdowns. Maybe you're standing at a crossroads. Or maybe, like me, you're finally choosing the scenic route. Whichever it is, I hope these words serve as your travel companion, your reminder that healing is possible, growth is real, and grace is available even here.

Let's keep going. Together.

First Turns

How We Learn to Navigate the World

I was twelve when Hurricane Gilbert hit Jamaica. The wind uprooted trees and tossed them around like toys on rooftops. My dad moved me and my sibling to his sister's home when the hurricane made landfall, leaving my mom and the rest of the family behind in the wooden house I grew up in. His sister's house was a place unlike any I'd ever known. The house was made of stone, unlike our old house, which was made of wood. It had running water, a flush toilet, and electricity, things I never imagined having in a home. For the first time, I didn't hear the cries from nearby funerals, which were a regular sound in my neighborhood. I didn't see poverty. I saw hope and possibilities. I didn't smell trash on the road. Instead, there was order and peace. And still, I felt entirely out of place.

That move was a detour on my road trip, a sudden, unexpected reroute that revealed not only a new environment but also a new awareness. Just like a road can suddenly change from gravel to smooth asphalt, so did my view of what life could look like. It was the beginning of me realizing that we don't all start from the same mile marker. And some of us, like me, begin the journey in a car running on fumes.

Looking back, I see how that one storm shifted my course. Hurricane Gilbert was more than a natural disaster; it was a moment of disruption, a turning point. Until then, my journey had been confined to what I had known: struggle, simplicity, and survival. But stepping into my aunt's home was like exiting unexpectedly onto a freshly paved highway. Everything felt foreign and advanced. And yet, with all its comforts, I didn't feel like the road belonged to me.

This experience planted an early realization that my life's road trip wouldn't be a straight line. There would be turns I didn't anticipate, intersections that would test my direction, and roadside stops that would show me how different life could be. But I wasn't ready to drive yet. I was just beginning to see the possibilities. That's the thing about driving to your appointment with death—you don't always know how far away the destination is, but every experience becomes part of the route. Some make you accelerate; others force you to break and sit in discomfort.

It was in that stone house, with indoor plumbing and quiet nights, that I first glimpsed what it meant to live with dignity and ease. And it was precisely because I had lived so long without those things that I felt like an outsider among them. That awareness, that tension between where I came from and where I found myself, was the beginning of me learning how to navigate not just the physical world, but my internal one too.

For a long time, I believed I had to become someone else to fit in. I didn't realize that my road wasn't about becoming someone new; it was about becoming fully myself. That truth came slowly, through life's lessons, detours, and quiet reckonings. It was on this early stretch of road that questions began to surface: What kind of driver would I be? Were there roads for someone like me?

I started noticing which roads felt safe, which ones didn't, and what it took to exist in places that weren't built for me. I was still a passenger, but I was alert, watching the signs, exits, and warning lights. Without knowing it, I was preparing for the day I'd take the wheel.

In my world, poverty felt like a lifelong sentence. It marked you in your clothes, in people's eyes, in the way you were excluded. I grew up feeling like I was already serving time. That constant judgment seeped into my thinking and shaped how I saw the road ahead.

Driving to My Appointment With Death isn't just about life's end; it's about how we keep going in spite of it. Every slight, every exclusion, every insult was painful, yes, but also fuel. I made a promise to myself: if I ever got behind the wheel, I'd drive roads no one thought I could. I'd go boldly where I wasn't expected to.

So I stayed in the driver's seat, even when my hands trembled. I studied the road. I listened to my own engine. Because if death is the final stop, then every mile before it is mine. And I plan to claim every one of them.

Once, I had a doctor's appointment and I went alone. I lay there on the table, and a group of student doctors walked in. No one asked me any questions. My doctor just proceeded as they looked, stared, and asked questions, and talked about me like I wasn't there. I felt invisible, exposed but unseen. So I did what I could. I covered my eyes, hoping they wouldn't see me if I couldn't see them. For a moment, I disappeared.

That experience taught me something lasting: how to vanish in plain sight. It was the discovery of a survival skill I would use many times. When no one acknowledges your humanity, you learn how to protect it yourself. That silence, that lack of care, changed me. And it reminded me that the waiting rooms in life often define us just as much as the destinations.

I didn't want pity; I wanted respect. I wanted to be seen not just as a body, but as a person with fears and feelings. No one paused. No one asked. That silence echoed louder than words.

That day, I learned what it meant to be unseen. Society doesn't always overlook by accident; it does so by design. So I began building armor from awareness. I became more intentional about when and how I showed up. I promised myself that although I may not be seen by everyone, I'll never again be invisible to myself.

I remember standing in front of the mirror at ten, tugging at my skirt, wondering why my body looked different from the girls in school or magazines. No one had to say anything—I felt it in glances and whispers. Compliments floated past me. Even when I tried to fit in, something always felt off.

So I got quiet. I chose clothes that didn't draw attention. If I couldn't be beautiful by their standards, I'd at least avoid ridicule. But silence isn't the same as acceptance. I wasn't just hiding my body, I was learning to hide my voice, my power, my presence.

In that moment, I became more aware of the road I had traveled up to that point. I didn't envy them; I simply didn't know how to join them. The verandah of my home became my silent observation deck, a place where I practiced being small and tried to understand what joy looked like when it wasn't interrupted by lack. Years later, I realized that even back then, I wasn't afraid to participate; I was afraid to be seen trying and failing. I didn't want my difference to become the punchline of their laughter.

It was one of those quiet turns on my road trip to selfhood, a brief stop that showed me how many of my detours weren't because I didn't want to engage, but because I didn't yet know how. That moment etched itself into my memory as a reminder: sometimes the scariest thing isn't the road ahead; it's stepping onto a path you've never seen anyone like you walk before. But now, with each mile I drive, I know that I am not only allowed to dance, I am allowed to make up the steps as I go.

In a way, my silence became its own kind of language, a quiet plea not to be seen until I was ready to be seen on my own terms. That moment, like so many others, became a mile marker on my road trip, a reminder that before you can fully show up in the world, you have to first make peace with the body you're driving in. It wasn't until much later, through love, motherhood, and education, that I learned how to stop shrinking. And when I finally stepped fully into myself, I realized that this body, this vehicle, had carried me further than I ever imagined it could.

I didn't have the words back then, but the truth was simple: I didn't feel like I belonged. Their joy felt foreign, like a language I hadn't yet learned. I didn't know the choreography of carefree happiness. Instead, I sat there with my hands folded tightly in my lap, silently rehearsing what it might feel like to move that freely. I wasn't just watching them dance; I was measuring the distance between their world and mine.

As I grew, I began to understand the mechanics of the road trip. I was no longer just a passenger. Childhood was the phase when I started noticing the outside world. I asked questions about the road, wondered about the signs, and mimicked the drivers around me. It was a time of imagination, curiosity, and discovery. I began forming my earliest ideas of where I might want to go, even if I was still years away from steering.

I noticed how others navigated their own paths, some with confidence and direction, others with uncertainty or recklessness. I studied them like roadmaps. Some were cautionary tales, others models to follow. I watched the choices they made, how they handled detours and disappointments, and I started piecing together the kind of journey I might want to take.

Every question I asked was a way of mapping the terrain. Why do we go that way? What happens if we stop here? Is there a shortcut? And every answer helped shape the compass inside me. I began to dream about places beyond where I stood, imagining life as something wide, open, and full of exits I hadn't yet explored.

This was the season of awakening, of realizing that I wasn't just along for the ride; I had the potential to choose. That realization was powerful. Even if I didn't yet have the keys, I knew one day I would. And that thought alone kept me curious, hopeful, and alert.

Those early years were filled with pivotal decisions: who I wanted to become, who I didn't. Each one became a marker on my internal roadmap, helping me prepare for the day I'd finally grab the wheel. In childhood, I learned to look, to listen, and to ask. Those early, observant miles helped me understand the road I was on and start believing that I could eventually shape where it would lead.

Then came adolescence, the learner's permit phase of life. I learned to drive. I got behind the wheel with shaky hands, full of uncertainty but hungry for freedom. I was excited but scared, like I was standing on the edge of a cliff and daring myself to jump. I wanted to prove something to the world—and maybe even more to myself.

I made mistakes. I ran red lights of advice, took wrong exits, bumped into emotional roadblocks, and sometimes ignored the GPS of wisdom from those who had driven before me. There were moments I thought I knew better, moments where I craved the rush of independence so fiercely that I missed the caution signs. But each mile, each misstep, taught me something new. I learned that even the wrong turns had value.

Adolescence is when you start to believe you've figured it all out, only to realize you're just beginning. I tested limits. I challenged authority. I tried on different versions of myself like outfits, trying to see which one fit. I crashed, sometimes into heartbreak, disappointment, even into myself. But I always got back up, sometimes bruised, but wiser. That stretch of road made me scrappy, resilient. It gave me muscle memory for recovery.

Looking back, that phase wasn't just about learning to drive, it was about learning to sit with uncertainty, to navigate doubt, and to understand that freedom doesn't mean directionless. It means choosing your path with intention. And those years, chaotic as they were, were essential miles in the journey titled *Driving to My Appointment With Death.* Because before you can make peace with the end, you have to wrestle with the beginning, and adolescence is nothing if not a battleground of becoming.

These years were filled with firsts: real friendships, heartbreaks, moments of rebellion, and tastes of new responsibilities. I still had people in the passenger seat coaching me, but my hands were now on the wheel. Every mistake I made was a wrong turn I'd have to reverse, but it was also a lesson in patience. Every small victory—passing a test, standing up for myself, choosing to say no—became a fuel stop, a reason to keep going. Some lessons came gently, others roared at me like an eighteen-wheeler in the wrong lane. But with each experience, I collected tools. I began to recognize emotional road signs: the red flags, the detours worth taking, the exit ramps to avoid. These tools didn't just make me a better driver, they made me a better version of myself. In time, I realized that having my hands on the wheel meant not just steering, but deciding who got to be in my car, which voices I let into my rearview, and what destinations I truly longed for.

Sometimes I tried to speed ahead, ignoring speed limits, desperate to grow up faster than I should. I wanted to be taken seriously, to escape the vulnerability of being in transition. I thought if I could just get there, wherever "there" was, I'd finally feel worthy, finally feel like I belonged on the road with the grown-ups. But life doesn't work that way. The road has rules. And when I tried to outrun them, I paid for it in heartbreak, in missteps, in moments of crashing hard into my own limitations.

Other times, fear paralyzed me. The wheel was in my hands, but my foot hovered over the brake. I was terrified of making the wrong move, of veering off into something I couldn't undo. So I'd stall. I'd stay parked in situations I'd outgrown or sit at emotional intersections for too long, waiting for a green light that would never come. It was a phase of trial and error, full of detours and restarts. But every turn, every mile driven, built confidence. Slowly, I realized that the wheel responded to my touch. I didn't have to be fearless, I just had to be willing to drive through the fear.

Eventually, I earned the right to drive alone. That transition from supervised learner to solo driver was both thrilling and terrifying. I now understood that the road ahead held both beauty and danger. I'd have to be my own navigator, my own roadside assistance. And though I still called home for directions, this stretch of the journey became mine to navigate. Every pothole and panoramic view was mine to experience. The mistakes no longer felt like failures; they became feedback. The victories, no matter how small, reminded me that I was capable.

Childhood and adolescence laid the foundation of my independence. These stages were filled with exploration, risk-taking, and the slow development of identity. The mistakes I made didn't disqualify me; they prepared me. This was my season of learning how to handle the road. And as I continue this long, winding trip toward my eventual appointment with death, I look back at those early miles not with regret, but with deep gratitude. Because without them, I wouldn't know how to navigate what lies ahead. Without them, I wouldn't trust myself behind the wheel.

One act of rebellion still makes me smile. In fifth or sixth grade, I placed a plastic frog in a teacher's bag as a prank. When she opened it, she screamed, and I was suspended. At the time, it felt like the ultimate thrill, watching someone so composed unravel, if only for a second, because of something I did. But that adrenaline rush quickly turned into dread. I couldn't tell my family, so I had a friend pose as my sister during the disciplinary meeting. Somehow, we pulled it off. We laughed about it for years, but beneath the laughter, did I learn something? I didn't fully understand what I had done until years later: I had been starved for attention. That prank wasn't just about humor, it was about making my presence known in a world where I often felt invisible.

That moment was a swerve in the road, a sharp turn that reminded me that life didn't have to be all weight and sorrow. Sometimes, it could be lighthearted and absurd. It also showed me that rebellion wasn't always about destruction. It could be a cry for acknowledgement, a request to be seen. That frog, silly as it was, became a symbol of my need to disrupt the script I'd been handed.

I dropped out of high school at seventeen years old. Years later, as a single mom with two kids, I went back for my GED. I failed four times. On the fifth, I passed. Then came an associate degree, a bachelor's degree with honors, and finally, completing a master's loan-free in just over a year. With every milestone, I found new layers of worth. That journey from the prank to the diploma became a full-circle stretch of road. What started as a desperate plea to be seen became a determined mission to define my own path.

Meanwhile, as I forged my future, I experienced another doctor's visit that changed me. This time, they asked to bring in student doctors. I said no. That might sound small, but it was a defining moment. I realized I had a voice, and more importantly, I had a right to use it.

That "no" became the steering wheel in my hands. That was the day I stopped letting people drive over my boundaries.

I didn't always understand my parents. But I see now that they loved us the best they could. They did what they knew, and they wanted more for me than they ever had for themselves. My environment didn't start strong, but it evolved. I grew up and shaped a better one for my children, thanks to the support from family and friends.

This is my road trip. And I am in charge.

The road wasn't straight, but it was mine. And I am still learning to drive it. Every wrong turn, every stall, every acceleration? I earned them. And now I steer with purpose.

Passengers & Pitfalls

The People Who Shape the Ride

On any great road trip, you pick up people, companions of all kinds. Friends, mentors, lovers, even strangers. Some ride with us for just a few miles, then quietly step out at the next town. Others stay for many exits, weaving themselves into our lives, maybe even riding with us until the very end. These human connections, brief or enduring, shape our journey. They add unexpected laughter to our long drives, offer comfort when the road gets tough, and sometimes even take us off course. But no matter the outcome, they're essential to the richness of the ride.

Some passengers show up when our tank is nearly empty, offering just enough encouragement to get us to the next stop. Others arrive when we're coasting downhill, adding excitement and energy to a ride already in motion. There are passengers who ask us to change lanes, to take back roads, to slow down and enjoy the view. And some, without even knowing it, help us avoid collisions.

We're not always prepared for who gets in. Sometimes, we pull over for people simply because we're lonely. We offer them the front seat out of habit or hope. We give them the map because we're too tired to navigate. But time and the trip itself teach us to be more discerning. We learn to ask: Who helps me drive better? Who makes the ride harder? Who uplifts, and who undermines?

Every person who climbs into our car brings something with them. Some bring wisdom, others bring warning signs. A few bring heavy baggage that spills into every corner of the vehicle. Some lighten the load just by being there. And yet, even the most difficult passengers have value. They teach us about our own limits, what we'll carry, what we won't, and when it's time to let someone off at the next stop.

The people who travel with us shape not just the journey, but the driver we become. And while it's true that we must ultimately steer our own wheel, the voices in our passenger seats often echo long after the ride is over.

There was one passenger I picked up when I least expected it. I was still nursing the wounds of a failed relationship, driving through what felt like emotional fog. My heart was bruised, not just by the breakup, but by the realization that I had been giving so much of myself to someone who never truly saw me. He got in the car at a time when I wasn't ready to drive. I gave him the map. He took us somewhere I never wanted to go. But I didn't realize until years later that I had handed him the wheel out of fear, not love. I was afraid to be alone, afraid to face the silence of my own thoughts. So I let him chart the course. It took hitting an emotional pothole to realize that the passenger seat does not come with driving rights.

The heartbreak unfolded slowly, in layers, in moments of dismissal, silence, and cold shoulders. It came in the subtle ways he made me feel small. I remember cooking dinner one night, hoping he'd notice the effort, hoping we'd sit and laugh like we used to. Instead, he ate quietly, barely looked at me, and left his plate on the table. That night, I cried into the sink while washing dishes. I was grieving the absence of joy in a house still full of noise.

But it didn't stop there. I remember planning weekends filled with things we used to enjoy, hoping they'd spark what we once had. But the interest wasn't there anymore. He was present in body, but not in spirit, swallowed up by silence. What had once been "us" felt like it had slipped away. I felt like a ghost haunting the relationship I once called home. Those weekends made it clear: I was holding onto a version of us that no longer existed.

Still, I kept driving. Through the tears, through the questions, through the self-blame. That relationship taught me something about myself: I was more comfortable giving than receiving. I had to unlearn the idea that love meant sacrificing my needs. I had to relearn what it meant to ride alongside someone, not behind them. I realized that just because someone is in the car doesn't mean they belong on the journey.

Then came a friend who changed everything. We met in a college class, two older students trying to finish what life had once interrupted. She was bold, warm, and spoke her truth without apology. We started to bond and foster a close friendship. We talked about our kids, our mistakes, our hopes. She didn't judge when I admitted I was terrified of failing. She didn't flinch when I said I still didn't feel smart enough to be in the room. Her belief in me became a mirror I didn't know I needed. That friendship was a safe passenger, the kind who adjusts the music, reads the map, and makes you laugh at the bumps in the road.

That friend didn't just ride along; she reminded me that I was worthy of good company. She showed up not just with kind words, but with action. She'd wait for me when I was running late, celebrate when I got good grades, and even challenge me when I doubted myself. Her presence was a kind of recalibration, a reminder that not everyone wants to take advantage of your journey. Some people genuinely want to see you arrive.

But not all passengers are easy company. I once had a friend who seemed supportive on the surface but was quietly steering me off course. She celebrated my failures more than my wins. She always needed saving, yet never showed up for me. Our friendship was a detour I stayed on too long. I kept driving out of guilt, out of habit, until I finally realized that not everyone deserves a seat in my car. Some passengers drain the tank. They take up space, consume your energy, and leave you wondering how you ended up so far from where you wanted to go.

Letting her out of the car wasn't easy, but it was necessary. It taught me that loyalty to others should never come at the cost of self-betrayal.

There are also the quiet passengers, the ones who ride with you without saying much but change everything. For me, it was a professor who told me my writing mattered. It was the cashier at the local store who remembered my name. It was my son, who once whispered, "You're doing great, Mom," after a long, hard day. These moments seem small, but they refuel you. They're like unexpected roadside stops with the best coffee and a view that makes you breathe a little deeper. They remind you that kindness, even in passing, can power you through the next stretch of the journey.

In my mid-twenties, I met someone and after just a couple of months, he came to visit me. As I watched him leave that Sunday, I had a feeling that I was never going to see him again. Not long after, I packed up and moved to be with him. It was spontaneous, maybe even reckless, but it gave me my two sons. The relationship ended, but that move turned into one of my biggest detours. I drove off course for love, and I wouldn't take it back.

My sons became my anchors. I realized I hadn't known love until I held them. Zach, my firstborn, taught me how to love freely, with open arms and no conditions. Josh, my second son, taught me patience, the kind that reaches deep into your spirit and rewrites your soul. They were the passengers I didn't plan for, but the ones who gave my ride its deepest meaning. They weren't just part of the journey; they were the destination that gave my wandering purpose.

There were moments of awakening in early motherhood. I got my first apartment at twenty-one. It was my own space—no rules, no curfews, no one to report to. I bought what I wanted at the grocery store, danced barefoot in the kitchen, and felt the intoxication of freedom. I was finally steering my own car with no one in the back seat telling me what to do.

But motherhood changed that. When I held my first son in my arms, I cried for a week straight. Not because I was sad, but because the fear was overwhelming. How could I be responsible for this tiny human when I was still trying to figure myself out? In those sleepless nights, rocking him back and forth, I realized adulthood was just improvisation with better posture. No one really knows what they're doing. Some just fake confidence better than others.

Romantic relationships, especially, have shaped my sense of direction. One taught me that passion without respect is like a car with no brakes. Another showed me that shared dreams are more important than shared zip codes. The man I moved to be with didn't stay, but he shifted my entire map. His brief presence rerouted my future, and I'll always be grateful for that. Sometimes, love doesn't last, but the legacy it leaves behind does.

I met some very interesting people. Some were just great to hang with, some I could call on no matter what. Some I had to let go so that they could grow and so that I could heal. These relationships didn't last, but they etched something lasting in me. They reminded me of my depth, my resilience, my ability to love despite the scars. While I waited for love to find me, nobody captured my attention, until one day one online comment led to a conversation and, six months later, a proposal. This pulled me right out of my comfort zone, like driving a rental SUV when I was used to a small sedan. A brief connection that reminded me I was still desirable, still vibrant, and deserved to be loved. Some of these passengers are not forever, but they each left a mark on the upholstery of my heart. They reminded me of my depth, my ability to rise again, and my refusal to settle for half-hearted love.

Looking back, I can trace each turn in the road to a person—someone who came along just long enough to reveal something I needed to learn. Whether through comfort or chaos, they pushed me further along the journey of becoming myself.

Reflecting on these relationships, I've realized how each one brought something with them: clarity, chaos, laughter, pain, encouragement, doubt. Some helped me expand my horizons, while others pulled me into dark corners of myself I hadn't yet explored. They taught me to set firmer boundaries, to listen more closely to my inner voice, and to truly believe that I am worthy of joy, not just survival. Sometimes, we're the passengers in someone else's car. We try to help them steer, to navigate their storms. But there comes a time when we must get back into our own car, wave goodbye, and find our lane again. I've had to do that more than once. It hurts every time. But it also set me free. This chapter of life, on this stretch of road, is about discernment. Who gets in? Who gets to stay? Who gets access to the vulnerable places inside me? I used to open the door for anyone with a kind smile. Now, I ask better questions. I listen to how people make me feel. I check their baggage before letting them in. I've learned to protect my peace like I would a precious destination. I no longer entertain passengers who drive with reckless words or honk their own insecurities into my rearview. I choose carefully now, and it's made the ride much smoother.

Every person who enters our vehicle brings something: a lesson, a memory, a new direction. Childhood friends may hop in early, filling the back seat with laughter, candy wrappers, and secret dreams. Teenage friends crank up the music and shout out plans for the future over the wind. The scenery during these miles is often bright, open roads, sunsets, and freedom. These are the easier roads, where joy feels just a stretch away.

But as we age, the road narrows. The terrain gets rougher. Adult relationships are like winding mountain passes, sometimes breathtaking, sometimes full of blind curves. These companions are more than passengers; they're co-pilots. They might help you steer through fog, challenge you at forks in the road, or point you toward detours you never saw coming. And while some rides are scenic and smooth, others teach you how to hold the wheel steady when storms hit.

Each connection shapes how we travel and what we see along the way. We get passengers who stay only for a few exits, leaving behind fingerprints on the glass and echoes in the seat. Others stay for long stretches, becoming familiar voices on the journey. But all of them change the ride.

There are also unexpected passengers, people we didn't plan to meet, but whose presence forever alters the journey. They're like hitchhikers we pick up on a lonely stretch of road: unplanned, often brief, but unforgettable. A teacher whose belief in us shifts our perspective. A stranger whose kindness sparks something in us. A spiritual guide whose quiet wisdom helps us make sense of the road's bigger meaning. These encounters aren't mapped out; they happen when we least expect them, sometimes when we've nearly run out of gas or are questioning our direction.

They come in like sudden changes in scenery: a quiet lake after miles of desert, a field of sunflowers after endless gray. They wake us up. They remind us that even if we think we know where we're headed, the road has surprises. Their presence may be short-lived, but their impact lingers like a song stuck in your head long after the radio is turned off.

These are the moments that whisper, "You're not alone." The ones that remind us the ride is not just about where we're going, but who we become along the way.

And of course, not all passengers are easy company. Some create conflict, distractions, or emotional traffic. They challenge our patience and judgment. Some drain our energy like an uphill climb with no shoulder to pull over. But even these difficult rides offer clarity. They teach us to set boundaries, to read the signs more carefully, to pull over and reassess who's in our vehicle and why. They remind us that not everyone deserves a front seat and that sometimes, the most loving thing we can do is let someone out and wish them well as we drive on.

Eventually, we realize that we're not meant to drive alone. Companionship is part of the design. It's the shared playlist during long drives, the inside jokes that lighten the mood, the guidance when we're unsure which exit to take. It's the comfort of knowing someone's awake beside you during dark stretches of highway. These relationships add meaning to our miles. They illuminate tunnels, soften rough terrain, and bring celebration to the mundane. The journey isn't just about reaching a destination. It's about who's in the car with us when we get there.

Real-Life Parallel

Relationships are among the most powerful forces shaping our lives. Friends, family, mentors, romantic partners, and even brief encounters all leave their mark. Some guide us gently like scenic byways with calming views. Others challenge us like steep hills that test our endurance. But no matter their role, each relationship contributes to our personal map.

Choosing who rides with us is just as important as the direction we take. Just like curating a playlist for a road trip, we decide which voices fill our space. We must ask: Who lifts us when the road gets bumpy? Who helps us stay awake when we're tempted to give up? And who brings joy to the journey simply by being present?

As in life, some passengers are meant for short rides, some for the long haul. But all of them, in their own way, help define the road we travel and the person we become behind the wheel.

The Sacred Pause

Why Rest Isn't a Waste

I used to believe that slowing down meant falling behind. That if I wasn't in motion achieving, fixing, producing, I was somehow failing at life. Rest felt like weakness, an indulgence reserved for people who hadn't earned their stripes. Pausing meant giving up ground, and in a world that constantly told me to push harder, to stay ahead, to prove my worth, I believed that standing still would make me invisible. Pleasure? That was a luxury for people with less to prove, people who didn't carry the kind of invisible load I shouldered. I thought I had to earn my right to joy, to peace, to softness. I carried the weight of always needing to be useful, needed, busy. If I wasn't serving someone else's needs or building toward some milestone, I felt guilty, like I was wasting time, wasting potential, wasting purpose.

So I chased busy like it was a badge of honor. I scheduled every minute of my day, filled every gap with another obligation, another project, another favor I didn't have the energy for but said yes to anyway. I convinced myself that exhaustion was noble. That if I just kept pushing, just held on a little longer, I'd eventually reach a magical finish line where I could finally rest. "One day," I told myself, like a mantra. One day, when I had accomplished enough, when I had nothing left to prove, when I had secured everyone else's happiness, I'd stop. I'd breathe. I'd let myself feel. But "one day" never came. It was always just out of reach, moving farther away the faster I ran toward it.

I dismissed the fog in my mind, the moments when I couldn't focus, when even small tasks felt like climbing uphill. I silenced the longing in my spirit, that quiet yearning for stillness, for meaning, for something more than the constant cycle of doing. I wore my burnout like a badge, proudly telling others how little sleep I got, how many things I was juggling. I mistook depletion for discipline. I thought running on empty made me strong.

But eventually, the very momentum I was so proud of became a runaway train. I couldn't stop, even when I wanted to. I didn't know how. I had spent so long performing strength that I forgot what true strength even looked like. My body and my soul couldn't take it anymore. And in the unshakable desperation I had tried so hard to outrun, something inside me finally pulled the emergency brake. The moment would seem unremarkable to an outsider. Nothing grand or dramatic. A trembling in my hands. A tear I didn't know I was holding back. And suddenly, I couldn't go on like that. I had reached the end of pretending I could outrun my own humanity.

There was a time I wore my busyness like armor. I worked two jobs, sometimes three if you counted the side gigs I picked up on weekends. I was enrolled in college, juggling exams and papers with closing shifts and early morning alarms. My calendar was a battlefield of color-coded commitments: appointments, obligations, promises I couldn't bear to break. And still, I found a way to say yes to every request for help. Babysitting for a friend who needed a night off. Volunteering for the community project no one else had time for. Attending every birthday party and family gathering, even when my body begged for rest. I told myself I could manage it. That I had to. That people were counting on me and I didn't want to let anyone down. I believed showing up for others no matter the cost was the only way to prove my love, my reliability, my worth.

I became an expert at performing "okay." Smiling when I was depleted. Saying "I'm good" when my insides were unraveling. I ran from task to task like a machine, convincing myself that if I just stayed in motion, I could outrun the exhaustion catching up to me. But one afternoon, after a shift that blurred into the next and a night of studying that bled into dawn with only two hours of fractured sleep, my body finally said, "enough." I found myself parked outside a grocery store, engine still running, hands clenched on the steering wheel, and I couldn't for the life of me remember why I had driven there. I stared blankly through the windshield, watching people walk in and out of the store, their faces blurred like a dream I wasn't a part of. I didn't have a list. I didn't have a plan. I didn't even know what I was doing anymore.

Then the tears came. Not loud or dramatic, just silent, steady, slipping down my cheeks like rain on glass. Not from sadness, not even from pain. But from something deeper. Emptiness. A bone-deep hollowness that no nap or meal or encouraging word could fill. I had run myself down to fumes, scraping the bottom of a tank I hadn't refilled in years. And the scariest part? I hadn't even noticed. I had been so caught up in surviving, checking boxes, meeting needs, earning approval, that I hadn't realized I was disappearing. Bit by bit, I was dissolving into a version of myself that existed only to serve, to strive, to prove.

In that car, in that moment, I wasn't a student or an employee or a volunteer or a dependable friend. I wasn't anything but still. A woman too tired to move, too numb to pretend, too empty to keep going. It was the first time I stopped long enough to feel how much I had lost in the name of being everything to everyone. And though it didn't feel like it then, that breakdown in the parking lot was the beginning of something. The moment that forced me to confront a hard truth: that managing it all was not the same as living. That being everything for everyone had left nothing for myself.

It was in that moment, raw, silent, and completely unplanned, that something inside me finally broke open. There were no flashing lights, no dramatic collapse, just a quiet reckoning that settled into my chest like a stone. I realized, with a clarity I couldn't ignore, that I couldn't keep living like this. That I wasn't built to run on empty. That my body wasn't a machine, and my soul wasn't a storage unit for other people's needs. For so long, I had treated myself like a tool, valuable only when in use, worthy only when producing. But in that still car, in the middle of a grocery store parking lot, surrounded by the chaos of everyday life, I felt the deepest stillness I had ever known. And in that stillness came one thought, tender and unyielding: "Enough."

That sacred pause didn't look like the curated images I had seen online, no yoga mat on a beach at sunrise, no neatly scheduled self-care weekend. It looked like a tired woman in a parked car, staring blankly out the windshield, rediscovering the sound of her own breath. It looked like me, stripped of pretense, finally realizing that collapse isn't failure, it's a message. A message I had been ignoring for far too long.

I remember one morning not long after that, waking up and feeling like I couldn't move. Not because I was physically sick, but because something in me had gone quiet. Hollow. I lay there, staring at the ceiling, my arms heavy, my chest tight with something I couldn't name. My limbs felt disconnected from my will. My mind couldn't summon a single reason to rush, to rise, to re-enter the grind. It wasn't depression exactly. It was depletion. Soul-level exhaustion. I had nothing left to give, and the thought of giving more felt impossible.

That morning, in that stillness, I asked myself a question I had avoided for years, a question I could no longer suppress: "What am I running from?"

The words hung in the air like a fog, thick and sobering. I didn't have an answer right away. But I knew the question itself was the turning point. For the first time, I allowed myself to sit with it. Not fix it, not silence it, just sit. I let the truth surface, uncomfortable as it was. And slowly, painfully, I began to see: I hadn't been chasing success so much as I'd been fleeing stillness. I feared what the quiet would reveal. I feared that if I stopped moving, stopped proving, stopped pleasing, I'd be forced to face everything I had buried beneath the noise. The regrets. The grief. The loneliness I didn't dare admit. The dreams I had shelved in order to survive.

I wasn't just tired. I was spiritually starved. And it took that stillness, that unplanned, unglamorous moment of reckoning, for me to finally hear the parts of myself I had silenced in the name of productivity. I had built a life that looked strong from the outside, but inside, I was withering. And now, the only way forward was to stop running and listen to the truth I had buried beneath all my doing: I deserve to rest. I deserve to be whole.

I gave myself permission to be whole, to laugh again, not performative laughter, but the kind that bubbles up from somewhere deep and real. It reminded me to breathe not just automatically, but fully, intentionally. It told me I could enjoy my life, not just survive it.

And when I really leaned into that mindset, something cracked open. I remembered what it felt like to wake up without dread, to walk slowly and not feel guilty about it, to sit in the sun and let its warmth soak through my skin without thinking about what I should be doing instead. I thought of the last time I sat at the park with my boys, watching them run freely through the grass while I responded to emails on my phone. That moment came rushing back with a pang of guilt and a new resolve: I want to be present, not just productive. I want to make memories, not just meet expectations. That morning, in the quiet of my room, I allowed myself to sob not out of despair, but from the sheer relief of letting go.

I turned off the engine, leaned my seat back, and let stillness wash over me like a warm breeze through an open window. The world kept moving, but for the first time in a long time, I didn't feel the need to race it. I let the quiet hold me. I took deep, deliberate breaths. I let the tension unclench from my shoulders, the panic drain from my chest. I felt the weight of invisible expectations begin to lift, like suitcases being removed from the trunk. I closed my eyes and listened not to the nagging of my obligations, but to my own heartbeat, steady and resilient. Slowly, I began to feel like myself again, less like a machine and more like a person. A mother. A woman. A soul with permission to simply be.

No road trip is complete without pit stops. We take breaks to rest, to refuel both physically and spiritually. Sometimes, a pit stop is a full retreat: a weekend away, a long overdue nap, a moment of surrender. But other times, it's something smaller: a few pages of a good book, an hour in the sun, music that makes you dance in the kitchen. A snack might be a joyful hobby. A nap might be a spiritual retreat. A deep belly laugh might be that favorite diner meal off the highway, the kind you never planned for but needed more than you knew. These moments don't just refresh us; they remind us why the ride matters. They invite us to slow down, soak in the view, and savor the grace that exists in the in-between.

We equate motion with meaning, mistaking constant forward movement for progress. But just like a car needs gas and a driver needs rest, our souls need moments of pleasure and pause. Without them, we don't just get tired, we forget. We forget what inspired us to take the journey in the first place. We lose connection to our inner compass. We start to mistake speed for purpose, and that's when burnout creeps in like fog on the windshield subtle at first, then completely blinding. It's in these foggy moments that the sacred pause becomes not just helpful, but necessary, our only way to pull over, wipe the glass, and see clearly again.

This is what I learned while writing *Driving to My Appointment With Death*: that life is not just about getting somewhere. It's about being well while we're on the way. Because when the destination is inevitable, what matters most is how we live before we arrive. The sacred pause is not a luxury; it's the difference between arriving depleted or arriving whole. It's how we make peace with the ride, embrace its beauty, and remember that the journey of this messy, miraculous, ordinary life is the point.

Rest doesn't always mean stopping entirely. Sometimes it's as simple as turning down the music and letting the silence fill the space, taking a break from the noise of expectations, of social media, of internal self-criticism. It can mean closing the laptop without guilt or waking up without an alarm. Other times, rest requires a more deliberate detour, pulling over completely, canceling plans, saying no without apology. It's choosing your well-being over your to-do list. These pauses are sacred not because they're elaborate, but because they're intentional. They give us the space to hear ourselves again, to reset our emotional GPS before merging back onto life's highway.

Pleasure is the spice of the trip. It's the unplanned roadside attraction that wasn't on the map but ended up being the highlight. It's the impromptu dance session at a rest stop when a favorite song comes on the radio. It's the perfect coffee from a small-town diner, the one that surprises you with its warmth, flavor, and familiar comfort. Pleasure is in the laughter that erupts in the middle of chaos, the kind that melts tension like sunshine on frost. It's in the spontaneous singalongs, the moments of silliness that remind us we're more than what we produce. It's the joy of hobbies that make hours disappear, the deep, soul-stirring conversations that linger in your chest long after the car is parked. It's pulling over to watch a sunset even when the clock says you're running late, choosing presence over productivity. These are not detours from the journey, they are the journey. They are the stories we retell, the fuel that keeps our spirits light and our hearts soft.

I remember once agreeing to coordinate a community event during a period when I was already emotionally and physically spent. I told myself I was strong enough, disciplined enough to handle it all. But when the event ended, I didn't feel accomplished—I felt numb. My body ached, my head pounded, and I sat in my car afterward sobbing, not from sadness, but from sheer depletion. That was the moment I realized I had confused self-neglect with strength. I was speeding toward burnout with no exit in sight.

Wise travelers know constant acceleration leads to breakdowns. Real strength lies in knowing when to pull over. It lies in acknowledging that taking care of yourself doesn't make you weak, it makes you wise. It means understanding that rest isn't a pause from life; it is life. Because when we finally stop, even briefly, we're able to see more clearly, feel more deeply, and love more freely.

Real-Life Parallel

Pit stops represent more than just breaks; they are sacred pauses, essential moments of rest, recovery, and delight. They are the quiet Sundays when the world softens and time slows down. They are the vacations that aren't about itineraries but about presence. They are the afternoons spent with loved ones doing absolutely nothing that could be marked as "productive" on a calendar but everything that makes life feel full.

Snacks along the road, literal and metaphorical, are the small joys we often overlook: the music that makes us dance in our kitchen, the hobbies that bring us back to ourselves, the kind of laughter that bubbles up unexpectedly in the middle of ordinary chaos. They are creativity without deadlines, humor that lightens heavy moments, conversations that restore instead of deplete. These joys are more than distractions; they're fuel. They remind us why we're on the journey in the first place.

Pit stops challenge that belief. They ask us to reconsider the pace and purpose of our travels. They invite us to slow down not just to catch our breath, but to feel it. To fall back in love with the ride, not just the road ahead.

And that brings me to the heart of this book: *Driving to My Appointment With Death*. The title isn't meant to shock or depress. It's meant to wake us up. To remind us that, whether we admit it or not, we're all on this journey with the same final destination. Death is the only appointment none of us can cancel. But if the destination is certain, then the journey, the way we travel, becomes the most important part.

Are we speeding through life, missing the beauty on either side of the road? Are we filling every mile with noise and motion, afraid to stop long enough to hear what our soul might say? Or are we making room for the pit stops, for the joy, the wonder, the pleasure that makes the trip worthwhile?

Because in the end, the goal isn't to arrive at our appointment exhausted and empty. It's to show up whole. At peace. Grateful for the road we've taken, and the stories we've gathered along the way. The sacred pauses, the belly laughs, the spontaneous detours—those are not distractions from the path. They are the path. They're the reason we drive at all.

So take the pit stop. Savor the snack. Turn up the music. Roll the windows down. Let yourself be filled, not just moved. Because how we live between destinations is what gives the journey meaning. And when that final stop does come, may we not be racing to it in a blur of burnout but arriving with our hearts full, knowing we didn't just make it to the end . . . we lived on the way there.

CHAPTER

05

When the Road Breaks

Detours, Delays, and the Wisdom of Struggle

Not every part of the road is smooth. Sometimes, it feels like you're finally cruising, sunlight pouring through the windshield, a good song on the radio, your path ahead clear, and then, out of nowhere, you hit traffic. The kind that doesn't budge. Other times, you miss a crucial exit and suddenly you're miles off course, heart pounding, GPS rerouting. You get flat tires, setbacks that leave you stranded on the shoulder with no spare and no plan. And sometimes, the engine overheats entirely, and you're forced to pull over, steam rising, your heart racing, wondering how you're going to make it through.

Life has a way of mirroring those unpredictable turns. Just when we think we've found our rhythm, life throws something unexpected at us: an illness that shifts everything, a heartbreak that leaves us breathless, a failure that humbles us, or a grief so deep it alters the landscape of our lives. These moments don't politely announce themselves. They crash into our calendars and routines, knocking the wind out of us, demanding attention we didn't plan to give. They delay us. They frustrate us. They interrupt our carefully mapped itinerary. And yes, they hurt.

But as much as we'd prefer a journey of smooth highways and perfect weather, these disruptions are part of the road. They aren't detours from real life; they are real life. They force us to pause when we would have otherwise sped past ourselves. They slow us down long enough to check in with our souls, to notice what's been pushed to the edges of our awareness. They remind us that we are not invincible and that our strength isn't measured by how fast we go, but by how honestly we respond when everything falls apart.

It's in these moments, stuck on the shoulder with no clear next step, that we often experience our greatest growth. When the noise fades and we're left alone with our questions, we begin to see with new eyes. We realize we've been pushing too hard. That we've ignored the warning lights of stress, fatigue, and isolation for far too long. We may come to understand that the road we were on isn't right for us anymore. Or that we've been driving toward a destination that no longer feels meaningful.

Sometimes we need those breakdowns to reorient. To ask for help. To rest. To surrender control. To listen more deeply to the parts of us we've silenced in the name of ambition or responsibility. These moments don't just inconvenience us; they transform us. They show us what we're made of and what truly matters.

So yes, we will hit traffic. We will take wrong turns. We will break down. But if we let them, these interruptions can become invitations back to our truth, back to our humanity, back to a version of the journey that isn't just about arrival, but about awakening. And that is a road worth traveling.

It's not a road free of trouble, though. Some breakdowns come out of nowhere, with no warning, no gentle build-up, just a sudden jolt that sends your world spinning. One minute, everything seems manageable. You're making plans, sticking to your schedule, doing your best to stay afloat. And then, like a tire blowing out at full speed, something hits: a sudden diagnosis that changes the way you see your body, your future, your limits. An unexpected layoff that guts your sense of security. A betrayal so sharp it takes your breath away, leaving you reeling in the wreckage of a trust you thought was unshakable.

These are the moments that drop you to the shoulder of the highway, hazards blinking, heart pounding, paralyzed by the question: What now? You look around at a road that kept moving without you, and you wonder how long you'll be stuck there. You feel vulnerable, exposed. Everyone else seems to be zooming past, their lives uninterrupted, while you sit in the stillness of something you didn't choose and can't fix right away. These breakdowns are loud, disorienting, and they demand your full attention, whether you're ready or not.

Other breakdowns, though, don't come with sirens or smoke. They creep in quietly, like a slow leak in a tire. You don't notice them at first. You tell yourself you're just tired, just busy, just in a rough patch. You keep pushing through. Keep telling yourself to be strong. But over time, the signs become harder to ignore. The mornings start to feel heavier. Your laughter doesn't reach your eyes. You become quicker to anger, slower to hope. You start missing pieces of yourself but can't quite name which ones or when they went missing.

This is how burnout enters—on tiptoe, disguised as productivity. It wraps itself in praise from others: You're amazing. You do it all. I don't know how you keep going. And so you keep going, even when the engine starts to sputter. Even when the oil light is blinking red and your internal GPS is screaming for a rest stop. Loneliness, too, can creep in this way, especially when you're surrounded by people but feel invisible. Especially when you're always the one holding it together for everyone else.

We keep driving through it all, convinced that stopping would mean failure. We silence the warning signs, blast the music louder to drown out the knocking in the engine, take another sip of caffeine, and call it self-care. Until one day, we can't anymore. The car slows. The gears grind. And something inside us, body, mind, and spirit, forces us to pull over.

That moment is terrifying. Because it feels like everything is falling apart. But what I've learned, what life has shown me time and again, is that sometimes, stopping is the most sacred thing we can do. Not because we want to, but because we must. Because our healing depends on it. Because something inside us refuses to let us break further.

Whether the breakdown arrives with a bang or a whisper, it changes us. It asks us to listen, to tend to the parts we've neglected, to reckon with what we've been running from. And in that reckoning, if we're honest, if we're gentle, if we're willing to be still, we can begin again. Maybe slower. Maybe different. But with more clarity, more compassion, more truth.

Because sometimes the emergency lights aren't a signal of failure. They're a cry for care. A holy interruption. An invitation to see ourselves not as broken beyond repair, but as worthy of tending, worthy of rest, and worthy of returning to the road whole.

Detours, too, are unavoidable. No matter how carefully we plan our route, how confidently we set our GPS, life has a way of putting up "road closed" signs when we least expect it. Sometimes we take a wrong turn, an impulsive decision, a relationship that seemed right but wasn't, a job we thought would fulfill us but slowly drained us instead. Other times, the road simply disappears beneath us. A plan we depended on falls apart. A door we were certain would open never does. And suddenly, we find ourselves rerouted through unfamiliar territory, watching the landmarks we expected vanish in the rearview mirror.

At first, detours feel like failure. Like punishment. Like life's way of saying, you should have known better. There's disorientation, disappointment, even shame. You wonder if you made a mistake, if you're behind, if everyone else is on the main road while you're stuck meandering through back streets you never asked for. The uncertainty can feel suffocating. You don't know how long the detour will last, and part of you fears you'll never make it back to where you were supposed to be.

But here's what I've learned: some of the richest parts of my journey have happened off the main road. Some of the most meaningful relationships, the deepest healing, the most transformative insights have come not from the path I planned, but from the one I never would have chosen. Detours introduced me to sides of myself I might never have met if everything had gone the way I expected. They showed me I was more resilient than I realized. That I could survive disappointment.

That I could begin again. That sometimes being lost is the only way to be found.

I remember once losing a job that I had built my identity around. It was a position I had poured myself into, one I thought would lead to long-term security. When it ended abruptly, I was devastated. The panic set in almost instantly. What now? I had no backup plan, no clear next step. I felt like I had been dropped off in a strange city with no map, no signal, and no idea how to ask for directions. But that forced pause, that off-course season, became the birthplace of new dreams. It led me to a path that had more meaning, more alignment, more freedom. I never would have taken that route on my own. I had to be pushed there.

It's easy to view these redirections as wasted time, as setbacks that robbed us of progress. But so often, it's in the waiting rooms, the long walks back from mistakes, the restless, sleepless nights where growth quietly roots itself. It's in the in-between spaces where we meet humility, patience, and perspective. Where we're stripped of what we thought we needed, only to discover what truly sustains us. These seasons feel still, but inside they are pulsing with transformation.

Breakdowns and detours are often inseparable. One cracks us open, the other leads us somewhere new. Together, they become the threshold between who we were and who we are becoming. And if we're willing to pay attention not just to the pain, but to the lessons underneath it, we begin to see that our journey was never just about efficiency or arrival. It was always about becoming. And sometimes, the long way around is the only way home.

In some cases, we can fix things ourselves. We pop the hood, roll up our sleeves, and get to work. We recognize the problem and know just what to do: refuel, rest, recalibrate. Maybe all we need is a quiet weekend, a deep breath, a shift in perspective, or a day spent tending to the parts of ourselves we've neglected. There's power in being able to pause, take inventory, and make small adjustments that keep us going. And when those moments come, it feels good. We feel strong. Capable and in control.

But other times, no matter how hard we try, the engine won't turn over. We stare at the dashboard, fumble with tools we don't know how to use, and feel the weight of helplessness settle into our bones. It's in those moments that we need to remember something that took me years to accept: asking for help is not a failure. It's a lifeline.

Sometimes we need a mechanic, a therapist to help us untangle the knots in our mind. Someone trained to see the things we can't, who knows how to diagnose what's stalling us and guide us through the repair process. Sometimes we need a mentor, someone who's driven this road before, who can say, "I've been here too," and help us chart a path forward with the wisdom of hindsight. Sometimes we just need a friend, someone to sit beside us on the shoulder of the highway. No pressure to fix, no judgment, just presence. The kind of presence that makes the silence less heavy and the waiting less lonely.

And sometimes, what we need is divine intervention, something bigger than ourselves. A prayer whispered through tears. A sign we didn't expect. A moment of peace that washes over us for no logical reason. Call it God, call it grace, call it spirit—whatever name you use, there are moments when the only way we keep going is by surrendering to something beyond our own understanding. I've had those moments. When nothing made sense, and I couldn't think or plan or push my way through. When all I could do was close my eyes and say, "Help." And somehow, help came.

There is no shame in needing others. No shame in saying, "I don't know what to do next." No shame in pulling over and admitting that you're not okay. In fact, those moments, raw, humbling, human, are some of the most sacred on the journey. Because they remind us that we were never meant to travel alone.

More often than we might think, the strongest thing we can do is reach out. Make the call. Schedule the session. Share our pain with someone. Because healing rarely happens in isolation. We heal in community. In connection. In vulnerability.

So if your vehicle won't start, don't sit in silence. Don't wait for someone to notice the hazard lights. Ask for help. Wave someone down. Open the door to support. It might just be the only way to get back on the road, and not just moving again, but moving with renewed strength, deeper wisdom, and the reminder that even when we break down, we are never beyond repair.

And then there is grief, the ultimate breakdown of the heart. Unlike other detours or flat tires, grief does not come with a clear fix. There is no quick roadside repair, no spare tire waiting in the trunk. Grief pulls us over with a force we did not see coming, and when it hits, it can feel like the entire journey comes screeching to a halt. The silence after loss is deafening. Losing someone who rode beside us for miles, who knew our rhythms, who sang along to our songs, who helped us navigate the twists and turns, leaves an emptiness that words cannot fill. Their absence creates a hollow in the passenger seat, a quiet that echoes in every turn we take without them.

There are days when it feels like we will never move again. When getting out of bed, let alone back on the road, feels impossible. Grief is not just sadness; it is disorientation. It is reaching for someone who is no longer there. It is continuing on without the person who made the road feel less lonely. It is remembering their laughter at a stoplight, or their silence when you needed it most, and realizing that the map has changed forever.

And yet, the road continues. Not in the way it did before, and certainly not at the same speed. We drive on, slower perhaps, more cautiously, with the occasional stop to catch our breath when the ache resurfaces. But we drive on. Because we have to. Because they would want us to. Because love does not end at the point of loss; it transforms. It becomes memory, legacy, echo.

I think about driving to my appointment with death not as a morbid declaration, but as an honest acknowledgment that we are all heading toward an inevitable end. We are all, in some way, making that slow pilgrimage toward a final destination. But the presence of death does not mean the journey is void of beauty. In fact, it sharpens our sense of wonder. It reminds us that every passenger, every pit stop, every view out the window is precious.

Grief teaches us this in the hardest way. It reminds us that time is sacred. That nothing and no one can be taken for granted. The people we lose become part of our story, part of the road itself. We carry them not only in our memories but in the way we live moving forward. The way we love. The way we forgive. The way we take nothing for granted.

Some days, I still glance at the seat beside me and feel the sting of absence. But I also feel gratitude for the miles we shared, for the lessons I carry, for the way their love still guides me when I am lost. Grief may slow us, reshape us, even break us open, but it never has the final word. Because as long as we keep driving, as long as we keep honoring their memory with how we live, they are still with us. Not behind us. With us.

And that, I have come to believe, is the quiet miracle of grief. That in the ache of loss, love remains. Love drives us forward.

Even as we make our way to our own appointment with death, we can do so with hearts that remember, that feel, that continue loving mile after mile.

Real-Life Parallel

Life's challenges, whether they crash into us without warning or wear us down slowly over time, test our resilience in ways we never imagined. They reveal who we are beneath the routines, beneath the carefully curated strength, beneath the masks we wear to keep moving forward. Some storms announce themselves in headlines: divorce, diagnosis, job loss, death. Others arrive quietly: a creeping sadness, the slow erosion of joy, a daily ache that settles into the bones of our existence. Whether sudden or slow building, these moments ask us not just to endure but to evolve.

Detours force us to let go of the life we thought we would be living. They interrupt the timeline we clung to, disrupt the version of success we once believed in, and reroute us through unfamiliar terrain. At first, they may feel like punishment, like something has gone horribly wrong. But with time and hindsight, many of us come to see that detours are not the end of the road. They are a different kind of beginning. They lead us to hidden blessings we would not have found otherwise. New strength. New calling. New depth.

Breakdowns are more urgent. They demand our attention. They do not allow us to keep pretending. They force us to stop and tend to what hurts, to confront what we have been avoiding. Whether it is physical exhaustion, emotional burnout, or the deep ache of grief, these breakdowns insist that we slow down. That we repair what has been neglected. That we ask for help if we need it. They may look like interruptions, but often, they are the very moments when healing begins.

Pain, loss, and hardship are not detours from life; they are life. They are not evidence that we have failed or fallen behind; they are proof that we are human. To love deeply is to risk losing. To try at all is to risk failing. To live fully is to eventually grieve. But these things do not mean we are off course. They mean we are alive. Fully, messily, vulnerably alive.

What matters is how we respond when the road crumbles beneath us. Do we pause and repair? Do we allow ourselves to feel the ache? Do we reroute and grow from it? Do we stop pretending everything is fine and start being honest about what is not? Sometimes the most courageous thing we can do is pull over and say, "This is not working anymore." And sometimes the bravest act is simply getting back in the car and driving forward, even when we are still tender from the wreckage.

Because even in our worst moments, even when we feel broken, lost, unsure of where we are headed, we are still on the road. And that matters. That means we are still here. Still breathing. Still choosing life, even when it is hard. And as long as we are still on the road, hope remains up ahead. Maybe not right around the corner. Maybe not in sight yet. But it is there. Waiting. Like morning light after the longest night. Like a rest stop after endless miles. Like laughter after loss.

That is what driving to my appointment with death has taught me. That it is not about avoiding the struggle. It is about learning to live through it with softness, with strength, and with the unshakable belief that no matter how rough the road gets, we are still moving. And that is enough.

Sunlight & Surprises

What We Find When We Slow Down

There are moments when we drive through breathtaking landscapes, moments so full of beauty, clarity, or joy that they feel like sunlight breaking through after a long stretch of rain. These are the graduations we once doubted we would reach, the weddings that felt like promises kept, the births of children who shift the center of our universe. They are the promotions that come after years of quiet sacrifice, the spontaneous yes to a new path, the conversation that changes everything, and the spiritual awakenings that show us who we truly are. These moments are like the scenic routes of life, the open roads where the sky stretches wide and the engine hums steadily, where we feel, if only for a moment, that everything makes sense.

I remember a moment like that after my son's graduation. It was the kind of day that exists somewhere between pride and disbelief, when you sit in a crowded auditorium, scanning a sea of caps and gowns, until you find him. Your child. Walking across a stage he fought hard to reach. Suddenly, all the years of packed lunches, late-night worries, report cards, and whispered prayers come rushing back, like a reel of memories playing in fast motion. The applause is loud, but inside, it is the quiet that overwhelms you, the hush of awe that fills your spirit as you watch him claim something that was once only a dream. I remember the way the sun caught the folds of his gown, the way his eyes searched the crowd until they found mine. In that moment, I rolled down the metaphorical windows of my soul, took a deep breath, and whispered, "Thank you, God, for this view."

That is what the scenic route feels like. It is the moment when we finally come up for air after a hard stretch of road and realize we have arrived at a place that makes the struggle make sense. It is a milestone that explains why we kept going, a pause where joy fills every corner of our being and gratitude becomes a full-body experience. It is the warmth of the sun on your face, the song that makes you sing without inhibition, the peace that is not loud but steady, like the rhythm of tires gliding over smooth pavement after miles of potholes.

Another time, I was sitting outside with a cup of tea, watching my children laugh in the distance, their voices light and unburdened. The air carried a faint hint of jasmine, and for the first time in a long while, I felt completely still. It was not because everything in my life was perfect, because it was far from that, but because I could feel joy even in the middle of imperfection. I was not rushing to fix anything, not chasing a list of things to do. I was simply there, breathing, smiling, living.

That is the essence of the scenic route. It is not a destination you map out, it arrives quietly in the spaces between chaos, in the exhale after a storm. It reminds you that not every beautiful moment must be earned through pain, although when it is, it often feels even sweeter. It teaches you to collect moments like these and tuck them deep into your soul for the days when the road feels long again.

When the journey becomes hard, I try to remember those pockets of peace. I remind myself that more will come, if I keep moving and keep believing. The scenic route is not about perfection or ease, it is about presence. It is about never forgetting the beauty that remains, even in the middle of healing and even in the middle of becoming.

These are the moments that make the hard parts worth enduring. They do not erase the pain or undo the detours, but they change the way we see them. They tell us, "It mattered. You made it. Keep going." They are not always grand or carefully planned. Sometimes they arrive quietly, in the form of a moment in the kitchen, laughter around a table, or the soft weight of a child falling asleep on your shoulder. But when they do, they remind us that life is not just made of struggle. It is also made of sweetness, of sunlight, and of open skies.

And we must not miss them, because these are the memories that will one day become our landmarks. They will be the moments we revisit when the road gets hard again, the ones that help us remember why the journey was worth it in the first place.

These are the stretches of the journey where life feels light, wide, and full of promise, where the weight we have been carrying seems to lift, even if only for a short while, and we remember what it feels like to simply be instead of constantly doing. It is as if the road opens in front of us, the sky expands, and for once, we are not bracing for the next bump. We are just driving. There is no rush, no tension, just motion and presence.

I remember one evening in the backyard when the sun began its slow descent behind the trees. My youngest was chasing bubbles, giggling as they floated and popped in the warm air. My oldest sat on the porch, earbuds in, nodding along to a song I could not hear. And I was simply still. No phone in my hand, no thoughts pulling me in ten directions, no guilt about what I "should" have been doing. Just that moment, that light, that peace. The grass was slightly overgrown, the dishes were probably still in the sink, and my to-do list had not disappeared, yet none of it mattered. I felt like the world had paused for us, so I could take in the grace of right now.

That is what the scenic route does. It slows everything down, not because the road becomes easier, but because we finally notice the beauty that has been around us all along. Time stops feeling like an enemy and becomes more like a quiet companion. Joy stops being something we have to chase or earn; it simply exists. It shows itself in the colors of the sky, in the laughter of someone we love, in the calm that fills our chest when there is nothing to fix.

Gratitude comes softly in these moments, not as a demand, but as a gift. It arrives like warm sunlight streaming through the windshield on a crisp morning drive. You feel it deep within you, in the way your shoulders relax and your heart opens. It is not the kind of joy you post for others to see or try to capture in words, because it is more than that. It is the kind that brings tears to your eyes for no reason at all, the kind that makes you think, "I never want to forget this."

These moments are not daily occurrences, but when they do arrive, they feel sacred. They remind us that even after long detours and dark tunnels, there are still stretches of smooth road and breathtaking views. And if we are paying attention, if we are willing to slow down, we will not just see them, we will let them sink in.

Scenic routes often appear when we least expect them. They sneak into ordinary days without warning. We may be trudging uphill, exhausted and discouraged, and then, suddenly, we round a bend and there it is—a view so beautiful it makes us stop. After all the striving, the uncertainty, and the whispered prayers, we are given a moment of clarity. A moment that says, "This is why you held on."

One such moment came during a therapy session I almost skipped. I was tired and convinced I had nothing left to say. But something nudged me to go anyway. Somewhere between the words I did not plan to speak and the tears I did not expect to cry, I felt a shift. I named a wound I had been avoiding for years, and instead of shame, what I felt was a surprising softness. My therapist did not try to fix me; she simply held the space. And for the first time in a long while, I felt lighter. It was as though I had reached the top of a long hill and could finally see the distance I had covered. That was a scenic route moment. Quiet, but powerful. A reminder that peace sometimes arrives in the most unassuming ways.

Sometimes it comes with a cry that changes everything. I remember the sound of my child's first breath, a tiny but powerful wail that filled the room and split my heart wide open. In that instant, everything shifted. All the waiting, discomfort, and fear faded into the background. I was witnessing a new life, a new chapter, a new us. It was a moment that expanded my soul, and I did not want to blink, afraid I would miss something sacred.

Other times, it is watching someone you love step into their moment of triumph. Seeing my son walk across that graduation stage, knowing the battles he fought to get there, was one of those times. His name was called, and time seemed to slow. That moment was a long, deep inhale after years of holding my breath. It confirmed that the uphill climb had been worth it.

Scenic routes can also look like moments of healing we barely notice until they are complete. One day, we wake up and realize we are no longer as angry as we once were. We pass a place that used to trigger tears and instead feel calm. We laugh without forcing it. We say "no" without guilt. We look in the mirror and no longer flinch. These are the victories no one else may see, but they are milestones all the same.

These moments allow us to see not just what is ahead, but also the roads we have already traveled. We remember the curves we have braved, the nights we almost gave up, and the mornings we kept going anyway. In that view, there is stillness, wholeness, and a grace that doesn't need to be earned, simply received.

And it all happens because we keep going. Because we do not turn back when the road becomes steep. Because we let ourselves hope, even when the sky is gray. Scenic routes are the reward for persistence, meeting us after we have walked through fire and still believe in light.

The beauty we witness on the scenic route is not just in the view itself, but in the story of how we arrived there. Every moment of joy is layered with the ashes of what we have endured. We appreciate it more because we know the detours we never planned for, the breakdowns that nearly made us give up, and the long stretches with no sign of progress. And yet, we kept moving forward.

That is what makes the scenic route breathtaking. It is the quiet victories that no one sees, the inner strength we carry without fanfare, the grace that met us when we had no more answers. When sunlight filters through the trees and catches our breath, it is not just a reward. It is a reflection of us, of the resilience that carried us here.

The scenic route is rarely about grand accomplishments. More often, it is found in the simplicity of a conversation with a loved one, the shared laughter at a dinner table, or a solo walk where our minds finally quiet. These are the deep breaths between storms, the golden hours of the heart. They remind us that beauty is still present, even in the chaos.

I think back to an evening when my boys were younger. We had no plans, no big agenda, just the comfort of being in the same space. The television murmured in the background while we folded laundry, passed jokes between us, and finished leftovers for dinner. Somewhere in that ordinary moment, something inside me exhaled. I was not rushing or striving. I was simply there. And that moment became one of the clearest snapshots in my memory.

The world often overlooks these scenes, yet they remind us that we are living. A phone call from an old friend. The smell of a favorite meal on the stove. A sunset that slows our steps. These moments ask for nothing but our presence and, in return, they give us clarity.

Sometimes, the most meaningful parts of our story are written during these uneventful stretches. Happiness sometimes lives in the calm moments, in the absence of urgency. If we are paying attention, we sense it clearly: this is joy, this is enough.

The truth is, we must be willing to slow down to see it. We have to resist the temptation to rush through life so quickly that we miss the view entirely. Scenic routes require intention, a conscious choice to be present, to notice, to celebrate. They are not about productivity; they are about perspective.

For me, slowing down began with reclaiming my mornings. I started waking up before the world asked anything of me. Just me, a cup of orange juice, and the sky shifting from deep blue to the pale gold of sunrise. Those hours became sacred. They reminded me that I am more than my roles, more than my responsibilities. That quiet was a kind of progress I had never recognized before.

Learning to be still was not natural for me. We live in a world that glorifies constant motion, where rest can feel like wasted time. It took courage to pause, to say, "This moment matters." I learned the importance of it when I realized my son had stopped sharing the details of his day. It was not that he did not want to talk; it was that I had been too distracted to listen. That awareness was like hitting a speed bump I had not seen coming. It forced me to reevaluate what deserved my attention.

Now, I treasure the moments when the house is still and I can hear my own thoughts. When my younger son hugs me just a little longer. When we laugh until we are breathless on the couch, watching something silly together. These moments will never make the news, but they make a life.

The scenic route invites us to trade urgency for awareness. It teaches that fulfillment comes less from doing more and more from noticing what is already here. Sometimes that means pulling over to watch a sunset, or saying yes to a walk with a friend even when the to-do list is long. These are the roads that shape both our schedules and our souls.

One morning not long ago, I sat on my sofa and watched the sun rise slowly, spilling light across the room. The house was quiet. My children were still asleep. And for the first time in weeks, I let myself breathe deeply. There was nothing grand about that moment—no milestones, no achievements. Just stillness. Just me, present and whole.

In that quiet, I remembered who I was before the deadlines, before the titles, before the pressure to prove anything to anyone. That sunrise reminded me that joy is still possible. That peace is often found in the pauses along the way to the finish line.

I sat there with a cup of tea, feeling its warmth seep into my hands. The hum of the refrigerator and the faint birdsong outside felt like a private concert meant just for me. In that pause, I forgot about trying to be anyone's boss, savior, or solution. I was simply a woman learning to be gentle with herself.

That morning taught me that presence must be an active choice to sit, to feel, to remember that I am allowed to slow down. That moments like this should simply be noticed when they come, that I do not need to earn them.

These moments matter more than we often admit. They remind us that we are more than our struggles or ambitions. We are human beings, created to feel wonder, to laugh until our sides ache, to delight in the ordinary. When we let ourselves live these moments fully, they ground us, they change us, and they make the journey worth every mile.

Real-Life Parallel

Joy and discovery are so much more essential than mere luxuries; they are necessary for the soul. Milestones, awakenings, and small moments of awe feed us emotionally and spiritually. They become the chapters of our story we return to again and again, the "remember when" moments that anchor us in both who we have been and who we are becoming. They make the climb worth it and the view unforgettable. Let yourself be moved by them. Let yourself be changed.

CHAPTER

07

In the Dark

Driving by Faith When the Lights Go Out

There was a season in my life when I was completely directionless. And I don't mean the kind of confusion where you're trying to decide between two good options, or where to move next, or what degree to pursue. No, this was deeper. I was spiritually lost. Emotionally empty. Drifting. I had no fire in my chest, no vision in my mind, no joy in my mornings. I wasn't dreaming anymore, I was just surviving. Even then, in the quiet places of my soul, I whispered prayers into the darkness, asking God if the road was still there beneath my feet. I could not see it, but I needed to believe it existed.

I remember waking up each day with this heavy fog pressing down on me. My body would go through the motions—shower, clothes, keys—but my spirit wasn't in it. There was no energy behind my eyes, no excitement for what the day might hold. Just exhaustion that sleep never seemed to fix. I was functioning, but I wasn't living. I'd smile when I needed to, answer emails, show up for others, but inside, I was unraveling thread by thread. Quietly. Invisibly. The kind of unraveling people don't always see until it's too late. I began to wonder if God saw me unraveling, and if so, why He was so silent.

It was more than burnout. More than being "tired" or "stressed." I was tired in my bones, tired in my soul. Tired in that deep-down place where hope usually lives. And that was the scariest part; I couldn't find my hope. I used to be someone who believed in brighter tomorrows, who looked for the lesson in everything, who held onto faith even when the odds were stacked against me. But somewhere along the way, after too many disappointments, too much pretending, too many nights crying behind closed doors, I stopped believing that things would get better. Still, somewhere deep inside, there was a faint ember, a stubborn belief that God might still be holding the map even if I had dropped mine.

And what made it harder was that on the outside, I was still showing up. Still responsible. Still "strong." But inside, I was drowning. Silently begging for someone to notice, for life to give me a break, for some kind of sign that I wasn't losing myself completely. I asked God for that sign more than once, though my prayers felt like they were bouncing off the ceiling.

I didn't know what I needed back then. I just knew I couldn't keep going like that. I felt like I was driving through thick fog, headlights barely piercing the darkness, with no sense of where I was headed or how much longer I could keep driving. I was lost, and not just lost in my circumstances, but lost in myself. I couldn't find the version of me that used to light up rooms. I couldn't find the voice that used to speak with conviction. I couldn't even find the tears some days. Just numbness. Just silence.

That was my night drive. The season where the road was real, but the view was gone. Where I had no GPS, no guiding star, no voice from heaven telling me what to do next. Just a steering wheel, a pulsing heart, and the faint, desperate hope that something, anything, might eventually shift. Looking back now, I can see that God was there in the passenger seat, even if I refused to look over, afraid of what I might—or might not—see.

I've spent years working jobs that didn't bring me joy. Positions that demanded everything from me—my time, my energy, my heart—but returned very little. Still, I poured myself in. Especially in childcare.

My very first nanny job was with a family of children, full of energy, full of needs, and somehow, full of a kind of light that made me show up every single day even when it was hard.

I was so committed to those children. I knew their favorite snacks, the songs that calmed them when they were anxious, and the bedtime routines that made them feel safe. I wasn't just clocking in, I was loving them, protecting them, guiding them in the little moments that would help shape the kind of men they might become. I showed up in the way I wish more people had shown up for me when I was a child.

But the woman I worked for—their mother—was cold. Unkind. Dismissive in that way that slowly chips away at your spirit. She made me feel like no matter what I did, it was never enough. Never good enough. Never right enough. There were days I'd leave her house and cry in my car, not because the work was too much, but because being invisible is a kind of violence people don't talk about. I stayed, not for her, but for those children. I stayed because they deserved stability. They deserved someone who saw them. In those moments, I would pray for patience, asking God to help me show up for the children even when every part of me wanted to walk away.

What she never knew was how much I carried quietly and chose not to release. I held stories and truths that could have shifted the road beneath her, evidence that might have changed the course of things. There were nights I sat with the thought of how easy it would be to hand over what I knew and walk away feeling justified. But I didn't. I couldn't. Adding to her pain wasn't the road I wanted to take. Compassion became my compass, reminding me that sometimes strength is not in what we say, but in what we choose to leave unspoken.

But I didn't. I walked away instead. Not because I was weak, but because I was tired of participating in cycles of harm. I chose peace over retaliation, even when it cost me. Even when my story never got told. Even when she got to walk away thinking she'd won something. She may never know the mercy she received, but I do. And I believe God knows too, because it was His whisper in my spirit that told me to put down the weapons I was tempted to use.

I carry that choice with me. Not like a badge, but like a scribbled note in the back of my soul: you could have, but you didn't. And sometimes, that's the kind of strength that never gets recognized, but matters the most. The kind that chooses healing over revenge. The kind that closes a chapter with dignity, even when you deserved justice.

And yet, that decision didn't come without pain. That season in my life felt like one long night drive. I was exhausted, unsure of what direction I was heading in, pouring myself out for other people's families while still struggling to figure out what my own future looked like. There was no map for it. No guide. Just me, moving forward in the dark, one act of grace at a time. Even then, I was beginning to understand that faith sometimes means moving forward without any visible confirmation that the road will hold your weight.

There was one moment that still sits heavy on my chest. It was one kid's birthday—a big celebration with decorations, catered food, and a custom cake that probably cost more than I made in a week. On the surface, everything sparkled. But underneath, the energy told another story. The tension in the room wasn't the kind that comes with a busy party. It was heavier, quieter, something deeper that unsettled me.

Later that weekend, I overheard the housekeepers talking among themselves. They didn't know I was nearby. Their voices were low, tight with emotion. They were talking about the cake. And what I heard made my stomach twist.

Out of retaliation for how poorly the children treated them and how the parents continued to ignore it, the housekeepers had spit on the birthday cake before it was served.

They laughed about it. Not from joy, but from a place of deep resentment and pent-up frustration. And I understood that laughter in a way I wish I didn't. It was the laughter of people who had been disrespected one too many times. Who had swallowed too much. Who had been made to feel small in a house that demanded their service but never offered them dignity. That day, they took power the only way they knew how.

Still, my heart sank. Not because I didn't understand the rage that led them there, but because everything about it felt toxic. Broken. Wrong. These children had learned early on that money could shield them from accountability. That cruelty could be dismissed as personality. That grown adults were theirs to command. And the parents, so caught up in their own worlds, didn't see, or chose not to. Time and again, I had watched those children speak to the staff with open disrespect. I had seen the eyerolls, the snapping fingers, the disregard. And time and again, nothing was done. I remember thinking, "This is what happens when love is absent and faith is not taught, when the only compass in a house is wealth instead of wisdom."

That was a tipping point. I felt sick imagining the family devour the cake with joy, completely unaware of what had happened. Not just because of what was in the cake, but because of what it symbolized. A house where people felt so disrespected, so invisible, that this became their only way to be seen. It wasn't just the children who were hurting people, it was the environment that raised them to believe they could.

I did ask the housekeepers about what I'd heard. They denied it, of course. Told me I must've misheard. That it was just talk. But their faces told a different story. And so did mine.

I didn't say anything to the parents. Not because I was afraid, but because I was done. I had given that household enough of my energy, my presence, my care. I had shown up day after day in good faith. And what I received in return was tension, disrespect, and exhaustion. As I walked away, I prayed for those kids, asking God to break the cycle before it became permanent.

I quit. Not with fanfare. Not with drama. Quietly. Firmly. I chose myself. And that decision, though painful, was one of the clearest I've ever made. That moment became my line in the sand. I realized then that working in toxic spaces, no matter how polished they appear, was costing me more than I was willing to pay. It wasn't just a job anymore. It was emotional erosion. Spiritual damage. A constant reminder that if I didn't protect my peace, no one else would.

That afternoon, driving away from that house for the last time, I didn't feel anger. I felt free. I was exhausted, yes. But I was also clear. It was as if God had whispered, "Daughter, the road you are on is not the one I chose for you. It is time to turn." Sometimes the most powerful thing you can do is quietly remove yourself from the chaos and refuse to return. Each job. Each chapter. Each paycheck. Each promise. They left me a little more fractured. Each one felt a little empty. And the saddest part? I kept showing up, thinking it would be different, that if I just worked harder, smiled more, kept my head down a little longer, I'd find the place where I could breathe. But all I found was exhaustion.

I worked long hours, sometimes past dark, sometimes through weekends without overtime pay. No bonus. No benefits. Not even a thank you. I clocked in early and stayed late, not because I was asked, but because I cared. Because I had pride in my work. Because I thought that maybe if I gave more, someone would finally see me. Value me. But too often, someone else took the credit. Someone who knew how to play the politics better than I did. Someone who spoke with confidence but didn't do half the work. I kept thinking, "Maybe next time it'll be different." But it wasn't.

Some jobs don't care about you. Not really. They just care that you show up. That you keep producing. That you meet their deadlines, hit their quotas, smile when you're tired, and stay silent when things feel wrong. They want your energy, your time, your commitment, but not your voice. Not your needs. Just your labor. And once you burn out, they'll replace you before your seat even gets cold. I began to realize that in God's eyes, I was not meant to be disposable. I was created for more than endless output.

What hurt the most, though, was watching people who came from the bottom—people like me—make it to the top and forget where they came from. Instead of extending a hand, they turned their backs. Instead of lifting others, they looked down on them. Sat in their high-backed chairs and acted like they didn't remember how it felt to be overlooked, underestimated, or passed over. They forgot the struggle. Or maybe they remembered and just didn't care anymore. And I get it, success changes people. But it shouldn't erase their empathy.

I've sat in meetings watching someone who once stood shoulder to shoulder with me suddenly speak to me like I didn't belong at the table. I've had supervisors who wore their titles like armor, using them to intimidate rather than inspire. I've seen what power does to people who were never given it before: they confuse respect with control, leadership with dominance. In those moments, I prayed for the humility to remember my own journey if I was ever given influence. And all the while, I kept working. Kept pushing. Kept hoping that something would change. But it didn't. Not in those places.

And that, I've come to realize, is what working in broken systems does—it doesn't just challenge your skills; it chips away at your sense of self. You start to question your value. You begin to believe the silence around your contributions means they weren't real. You start to fade slowly, quietly, from the inside out. And yet, somehow, I kept going.

That was my night drive. No clear path. No destination in sight. Just me behind the wheel, driving in the dark, exhausted and unseen, hoping that at some point the sun would rise again. Faith, in that season, was like trusting the road existed even when my headlights barely lit the next few feet. There came a time when I couldn't keep doing it.

The grind. The pretending. The constant effort to hold it all together while silently falling apart. The work wasn't just demanding, it was dismantling me. Gradually. Subtly. In ways I didn't even recognize until I couldn't fake it anymore.

I was tired in a way sleep couldn't fix. Tired of giving more than I had. Tired of smiling when I wanted to scream. Tired of running on fumes while telling everyone I was fine. Tired of showing up to jobs that drained me, relationships that diminished me, and spaces that never saw me. And still, after all that effort, I was coming up short. Financially. Emotionally. Spiritually. It felt as though I was stranded on the side of life's highway with the gas light blinking, and the only thing keeping me from breaking down completely was whispering, "Lord, please don't let me stall here."

That's when I hit rock bottom. I quit my job with no backup plan. No security net. Just a knowing in my gut that if I didn't stop, something in me was going to break that I couldn't put back together. I remember sitting in silence—true silence—for the first time in years. No background noise. No to-do list. Just stillness and the echo of the question I didn't want to answer: How did I get here?

I didn't have an answer. Just exhaustion. Just grief. Just the sobering realization that I had betrayed myself over and over again by staying in places that hurt me. By working in systems that didn't care. By shrinking and stretching and overperforming, trying to prove I was worthy of a life that never seemed to show up.

That silence didn't feel like peace. It felt like exposure. I was stripped of every distraction. Alone with the truth I'd been avoiding. I told God I felt abandoned, yet in that stillness, a flicker of trust told me He was still in the driver's seat, even if I couldn't see the road.

That was my hotel moment. I didn't check into a literal hotel, but I did what weary travelers do when they can't drive another mile: I pulled over. I stopped. I chose stillness because my soul demanded it. And somewhere deep inside, I sensed that rest would be the only way forward, though I didn't yet know what that rest would look like. And then I did something I hadn't done in years: I booked a solo trip.

I flew to Jamaica to spend time with my grandmother, the one person who always reminded me who I was underneath all the roles and expectations. I didn't go for a vacation. I went for healing. I needed to breathe again. To feel again. To remember the version of me who existed before burnout became my baseline.

She was in a nursing home, and she had made peace with that. The daily activities with her peers gave her a sense of community and belonging. Her days unfolded slowly, almost sacred in their rhythm. I would walk in with food she loved, and her face always lit up when she received her pocket money. She loved God deeply and never missed a chance to remind me of how merciful He is. We stayed up late talking about life, love, and what truly matters. I watched her move without hurry, without performance, without apology. There was grace in her pace, wisdom in her simplicity. In those moments, it felt as though God was speaking through her, giving me permission to rest, to loosen my grip, and to trust Him with what I could not control.

And something in me started to thaw. I realized I'd been living in survival mode for so long, I didn't even recognize safety when I finally had it. In that quiet space—no deadlines, no pressure—I started to feel again. Not the frantic emotions of burnout or panic, but the gentler things I had lost: gratitude, comfort, presence. I started to remember who I was without a job title. Without a calendar full of tasks. Without the weight of pretending.

That trip became a balm for my soul. A reset. A retreat. A lifeline. I didn't know it at the time, but she would pass away later that same year. That trip turned out to be our final days together. And now, when I think of that season, I don't remember what I missed at work or who didn't understand my decision. I remember my grandmother's hands slicing fruit. I remember her voice humming in the kitchen. I remember the warmth in my chest when she looked at me and said, "You're tired. Rest."

That was the real gift: the invitation to stop striving and start healing. It was God's reminder that His yoke is easy and His burden is light, and that even the longest night drive eventually gives way to morning. Because rest isn't a reward. It's right. Stillness isn't laziness. It's sacred.

That was the moment I began to learn: healing doesn't always look like productivity. Sometimes it looks like Jamaica. Like a quiet kitchen. Like the sound of your grandmother humming while the world keeps turning. Sometimes, it looks like pulling over on life's highway and finally, finally, listening to your soul.

Since then, I've had other hotel moments. Times when I withdrew emotionally, not out of weakness, but out of necessity. I've pulled back when I was breaking. I've sat alone in my room, in my car, in quiet places where the world stopped long enough for everything I'd been suppressing to rise to the surface. And in those moments, those nights, I came face to face with the truth: we are all running from something. And when the noise stops, we finally hear what it is.

Silence has a way of confronting you. It shows you how little the world's approval matters. It reminds you that we came here with nothing and we'll leave with nothing, and that the things we chase so feverishly often steal the joy from the journey itself. The money. The titles. The image. The illusion of "making it." None of it means anything if we lose ourselves in the process.

I've been in that dark car, headlights barely reaching the road ahead. I've driven by faith when I couldn't see a single thing clearly, just trusting that the road still existed beneath my wheels. Trusting that God was still guiding. Trusting that my destination hadn't disappeared, even if I had no idea how close or far it was. And I've learned that in the journeys we can't see, faith is the GPS that keeps us moving, guiding us mile by mile until the light returns.

And I've stopped at the "hotels"—the moments of collapse, of pause, of deep, soul-level rest. Not because I'm weak, but because I finally understood I'm human. And humans need time to heal. Now I know that every road, no matter how dark, is part of the sacred trip we're taking home, and every pause is a holy reminder that the Driver has never left us.

The Ones Who Ride With Us

Love, Legacy, and Letting Go

Some passengers are lifelong. Family. True friends. They sit in the car with us not just during the highlight reels of life, but in the in-between spaces too. Sometimes we ride together in silence, letting the rhythm of the road fill the gaps in conversation. Other times, they're belting out old songs with us, turning the drive into a joyful memory. And yes, sometimes they bicker over the route, question the directions, or try to grab the aux cord. But through it all they are there. Present. Willing. Consistent. Their mere presence, whether loud or quiet, shifts the entire energy of the ride. They may not be driving, but they influence how we drive: how fast we go, how carefully we navigate, whether we feel brave enough to take the next turn. Their love becomes the reason the car feels like home, not just a vehicle.

These companions don't just ride along, they become part of the map itself. They shape the rhythm of our journey with their laughter, their advice, their wordless understanding. They've witnessed the detours we didn't expect, the breakdowns that left us sobbing on the side of the road, the scenic routes we almost missed, and the pitch-black nights when we couldn't even see the next mile. And still, they stayed. Not because they had to but because love said, "I'm not getting out." From the start, I have learned that not every passenger will stay for the whole trip, and some will leave long before we are ready. This chapter holds both realities: the joy of those who remain and the ache of those who drift away or must be released.

They've seen us strong. They've seen us scared. They've seen us messy and magnificent. They've cheered at our victories and sat with us in heartbreak. And in a world that often celebrates who walks away, these are the ones who stay. Their presence doesn't always fix the road but it reminds us we don't have to travel it alone. Their consistency becomes more than comfort; it becomes our anchor. A steadying force that keeps us from drifting too far into isolation, too far into despair. Because when life goes dark, and the GPS stops working, just knowing someone is still in the seat beside you is sometimes enough to keep going. And for me, knowing God is also in the car, even when I cannot see Him, is the constant reassurance that I will find the road again.

Family may be biological or chosen. For me, I've been blessed to always have my mom, dad, and siblings nearby. They've been the kind of family who show up in quiet ways. Not always with grand gestures or deep conversations, but by simply being there. Just the presence of them has often been a lifeline. A subtle comfort.

They've seen parts of my struggle, small pieces that peek through the cracks when I'm too tired to hold it all together. But the deepest parts? The parts that ache the most? I've kept those to myself. Not because I don't love or trust them. But because somewhere along the line, I convinced myself that they wouldn't understand. That if I shared all the doubt, the fear, the loneliness, it would just make things heavier. So I put on a smile. I carry the weight without complaint. I nod and say, "I'm fine," even when I'm unraveling. Sometimes I have whispered those unspoken aches only to God, trusting He could hold the weight without judgment.

There have been so many days when I've felt like I was walking through a storm without an umbrella. When my heart was breaking and I still had to show up. Still had to work. Still had to smile. And my family would be there, maybe watching TV in the next room, maybe laughing in the kitchen, maybe calling to check in. They didn't always know I was barely holding it together, but their presence made it just a little easier to keep going.

I remember one day in particular when everything felt like too much. I had just left a job that drained me completely. I was emotionally worn down, physically exhausted, and spiritually empty. I went home, walked straight into my bedroom, and sat on the edge of the bed. I didn't cry. I didn't talk. I just sat there. My older son passed by the room and looked in. He didn't say much, just gave me a slight nod and said, "You good?"

I wanted to say no. I wanted to scream that I wasn't. But instead, I just nodded back. And he kept walking. And somehow, that moment stayed with me. Not because it fixed anything. It didn't. But because it reminded me that I wasn't completely alone. Even when I was silent. Even when I was tired. Even when I couldn't explain what I was feeling. In that stillness, I felt a gentle nudge from God, as if He were saying, "I see you, even when no one else does."

Sometimes, that's what family is. Not the solution. Not the savior. Just the steady background noise of people who keep showing up. They don't always know what to say. They don't always know how to help. But they stay. And their staying becomes a kind of love. A quiet, unspoken kind that doesn't demand explanation. And maybe that's enough. Maybe love doesn't always have to fix or understand or explain. Maybe sometimes it just has to stay.

Yet, family has also disappointed me. And I say that with a full heart, not a bitter one. I've had moments too many to count when I expected more. Moments when I gave so much of myself, stretched beyond what was reasonable or fair, hoping someone would see me and meet me halfway. But they didn't. And the silence on the other side of that hope? It was deafening.

There's a particular kind of ache that comes when you realize the people you love most might not be capable of loving you back in the way you need. It's not obvious. It doesn't always come with yelling or arguments. Sometimes it comes in the form of absence. Missed calls. Words never spoken. Support that never arrives. You're standing on the side of the road, your hazards blinking, and you thought they'd be the ones to pull over. But no one comes.

That kind of disappointment doesn't just sting, it stays. It settles in your chest like a heavy grief. It makes you second-guess whether you should expect anything at all. Should you keep giving? Should you keep loving? Should you keep hoping someone will one day turn around and say, "I see you. I appreciate you. I've got you."

I learned the hard way that just because you love deeply doesn't mean people will love you back the same way. That just because you show up doesn't mean they'll notice. And that kind of realization can change a person. It can harden your heart if you let it. It can make you retreat, close the door, put up walls that say, "I'm safer alone." I've felt that pull. I've felt that temptation to isolate myself emotionally. To believe that no one was meant to understand me, and maybe I was just made to carry it all alone.

But I also know that kind of thinking makes the road unbearable. Bitterness adds weight to the journey. And when you're already tired, already running on fumes, that's a weight you can't afford to carry. So I've had to learn something that doesn't come naturally to me. I've had to learn how to forgive. How to let go, not because they asked for it, and not because they deserved it, but because I deserved to be free. I deserved to move forward without resentment riding in the passenger seat. I asked God to help me loosen my grip without hardening my heart, to teach me how to love without losing myself.

There are moments that stick with you long after they're over. One in particular shifted my entire understanding of what family really means. I was spending time with a friend's family, not a planned event, just a regular afternoon. We were in the kitchen cooking together, laughing, passing ingredients back and forth. Their conversations were open, gentle, even when they disagreed. There was a softness in how they corrected each other, a closeness in how they teased. And it hit me right there in the middle of all that noise and laughter. Something in me paused. I realized that what I was witnessing was not perfection, but presence. Support that was natural. Unconditional. Fierce.

And I knew, in that exact moment, that I didn't have that kind of rhythm in my own family. Not in that same way. I had love, yes. I had people who showed up in their own way. But not this. Not the kind of ease that comes from being truly known and accepted, flaws and all. That realization cut deep. It wasn't just jealousy, it was grief for something I'd never had but suddenly deeply understood.

But it also opened something in me. It reminded me that family isn't just the people who share your blood. It's not just about who's there when you're born or who shares your last name. It's about who shows up for you. Who listens. Who sees you, not just the version of you that performs well, that gets things done, that holds everyone else up but the version that's tired, that's confused, that's messy. I began to see that the ones who ride with me are those who choose me with intention, much like God Himself chooses to stay near even in my messiest moments.

That experience made me look at my own relationships differently. It made me both grateful for what I have and honest about what I still need. And more than anything, it made me redefine who gets to sit in the car with me on this road trip of life. Not everyone gets a seat just because they've been around. Presence is not the same as connection. And connection, I've learned, must be mutual.

Now, when I think about family, I think about consistency. About trust. About effort. I think about who checks in when they don't need anything. Who remembers your wins and your losses. Who claps for you even when they're struggling too. Who pulls over when you break down and sits with you in the dark, even if they can't fix what's broken.

I still love my family. I always will. But I no longer expect them to be everything I need. That was too much pressure for them and too much pain for me. Now, I let people be who they are, and I build my community around what's real, not what I wish it could be.

And that shift? That letting go? It's been one of the most healing parts of my ride. Redefining who belongs in my inner circle has become a part of my daily life. I've had to release people I love because they couldn't love me the way I needed. I've had to let go of the fantasy of what family is "supposed to" look like and accept the reality of what I have and what I deserve.

One of the hardest family-related heartbreaks I faced was being let down by someone I trusted deeply, a close family member who I believed would have my back, who I thought would show up for me the way I had always shown up for them. That moment didn't just sting, it knocked the wind out of me. It was one of those times when you feel like you've been driving with someone for miles, only to realize they've been asleep in the passenger seat the entire time.

But on the other side of that pain came a powerful awakening: I don't need everyone in the car to understand the route, I just need them to respect the journey. And in those moments when my heart still aches over that loss, I have prayed for God's help to keep my spirit soft and my road open to those He sends to ride beside me.

I do have friends who've become family. People who show up, not out of obligation, but out of love. They are reliable. They cheer me on without envy or judgment. They have earned their place beside me with trust and consistency. It's not about how long you've known someone, it's about how they make you feel when your tank is empty. These friends know when to bring gas and when to simply sit with me in the breakdown. They never ask me to be more than I am. They just love me, as I am.

I've lost people who were key to my journey: my cousin and my grandmother. They are passengers whose voices still guide me from the back seat, gone in body but riding with me in spirit. My cousin taught me that we don't have to fear death. That we can accept it peacefully, like an inevitable stop on the route. In his final days, he was so at peace knowing that he was going to die; he was positive about his life ending without fear, just honesty. That stayed with me. He reminded me to live, but also to prepare to let go. I often think of his calm as God's gift to me through him, a living example of what it means to meet the end of the road with courage.

My grandmother gave me the power to believe. In myself. In love. In possibility. She was soft in all the ways the world is hard. Being in her presence was like driving through the calmest, most sunlit stretch of highway. She moved slowly, intentionally. She didn't rush through her days and that rhythm taught me to slow down too. To trust the timing of life. In the days after she passed, I prayed for God to help me carry her wisdom forward, to let her voice still whisper directions when I feel lost. Her death was a hard curve in the road, but her memory still rides with me.

Losing them both changed the ride. My cousin and my grandmother were more than just passengers in my life. They were voices I trusted, hearts I leaned on, and souls that made the journey feel less lonely. Their absence created a kind of quiet I hadn't known before. Not the peaceful kind of quiet, but the kind that echoes in the spaces where laughter used to live. After they were gone, I started to pay more attention. To who was in the car with me. To who I let sit close. To who I gave access to my heart. I began to ask God to help me see clearly who He intended to ride with me in this season, and who I needed to release so I could keep moving forward in peace. I started asking myself, who has earned their seat? Who brings peace instead of pressure? Who can sit with me in silence and still make me feel understood?

Losing them taught me to listen differently. To love with more intention. To hold people tighter while I have them, but also to let go sooner when I need to. Both of those things can be true at the same time. You can love someone deeply and still know when it's time to loosen your grip. That kind of maturity didn't come easy for me. I've always been someone who tries to fix things, to hold on longer than I should, to believe that effort can repair anything. But over time, I've come to understand that sometimes, effort is not the answer. Sometimes, the most loving thing you can do is let go. And in those moments of letting go, I whisper a prayer: "Lord, help me loosen my grip without hardening my heart."

Yes, love has meant letting go. Not because I stopped caring. Not because I was angry. But because I finally got clear. Clear about what I needed. Clear about how much I had given. Clear about how staying was starting to cost me too much.

I've loved people with my whole heart and still had to walk away. Our roads had split, even though they weren't bad people. We had grown in different directions. And trying to drag someone along a path they no longer fit on, or one I no longer belonged to, was only hurting us both.

It's one of the hardest things to admit. That holding on is doing more harm than good. That what once felt like home now feels like a weight. But I've learned that love isn't just about sticking it out at all costs. Real love, honest, healthy love sometimes means saying, "We've come as far as we can together." And then letting go with grace. I have learned that God sometimes closes a chapter to protect us, not to punish us. To free both hearts for the roads ahead.

Letting go showed me that love can still be full of gratitude, even when it ends. It can still be sacred, even if it doesn't last forever. I've had to say my reluctant goodbyes to people who once felt like everything. I've had to sit in my car, hands on the wheel, eyes full of tears, knowing that I was about to drive off without someone I thought would always be beside me. And in that moment, I have felt God's steady presence in the seat beside me, reminding me I am never truly alone.

And still, I drove on. That is what growth sometimes looks like. Forget loud exits and slammed doors. It can be simple understanding. A soft goodbye. A thank you for the miles we shared. And then, turning onto a new road with your heart intact. Maybe still healing. But intact.

The ones who ride with us don't always stay for the whole trip. Some leave without warning. Some quietly drift away over time. And some, we let go not with bitterness, but with love. That's the rhythm of the journey. People come and go. Some exits break us. Others free us. But every person who sat beside us for a season left an imprint. A story. A lesson. A memory that rides along with us, even when they no longer do.

And those who remain, whether through blood, bond, or choice, become the steady hands that remind us we are not alone. Not truly. Not in the ways that matter most. They are the ones who bring us water when we've run dry. Who laugh with us when we find a stretch of open road. Who sit quietly when words aren't enough. They don't always have answers, and they don't need to. Their presence is the comfort.

Family and community are the constants that help define the landscape of our lives. Whether they show up loudly with celebrations and support, or quietly with a call, a meal, a ride, love has a way of anchoring us. None of us are perfect. No relationship is. But the people who stay, who choose us over and over again, help carry the weight of this journey.

When the storms come—and they always do—these are the ones who become our shelter. They don't need to drive the car. They just need to be in it. That alone is sacred. Because every mile we travel with someone, whether they stay for the whole route or just a few exits, changes how we show up for the journey ahead.

And in those quiet stretches of road, when everything is uncertain and the future is just a blur on the horizon, their love hums beside us like background music. Familiar. Steady. Comforting. This is what makes the journey worth taking. The ones who ride with us. And the ones we carry in our hearts, long after the road has changed.

CHAPTER

09

Looking Back to Go Forward

The Power of Honest Reflection

As we get older, we start glancing in the rearview mirror more often. We reflect on the roads we have taken, the ones we avoided, and the ones we wish we had not. Some of those roads were smooth, others were filled with potholes we did not see coming. There were times we took the scenic route on purpose, and times we wandered off course without realizing it. But every road added something to the journey. Every mile gave us a memory, a lesson, or a scar.

We begin to see the faces of passengers who are no longer with us, some who exited at the last rest stop, some we let go of at the toll booth, and some who vanished in the fog. Their absence echoes in the empty passenger seats, but their impact remains. The rearview mirror does not change the road behind us, but it helps us appreciate the ride. It becomes a sacred place of memory, a place where we honor who we were, who we loved, and who we are becoming. Sometimes it even reminds us of the unexpected hitchhikers we picked up, the ones who offered wisdom at a crossroads or made us laugh during a season when joy was hard to find, just as I shared in earlier chapters.

Reflection is one of the gifts of age. As our pace slows, our vision extends backward as much as it does forward. We start seeing how the smaller decisions, the quick left turns and the long pauses at intersections, shaped the rest of our journey. We begin to understand the significance of certain exits, how a choice we made in our twenties shaped the rest of our path, how a seemingly random stop turned into a defining detour, or how a brief encounter left a lifelong impact.

We start to notice that the things we once rushed past now call us to pause. The loud ambitions of youth grow quieter, and what rises in their place is the gentle wisdom of hindsight. In the rearview mirror, we do not just see events, we see meanings. We start connecting the dots between heartbreak and growth, between struggle and strength. We realize that the road we thought was a mistake may have been the very one that led us to something beautiful.

Looking back is no longer about regret; it becomes a search for clarity, for understanding, for grace. We begin to grasp how the hurried dreams of our younger years were just starting lines, not finish lines. There is something tender about the way age teaches us to slow down. Our younger selves often raced toward success, love, and belonging as if life were a checklist. But now, looking in the mirror, we see that the real treasures were in the pauses, the people, and the perseverance. Time has this way of polishing the rough edges of memory until all that remains is meaning. We start to see our past not through the lens of failure, but through the lessons it left behind.

We remember the laughter, those late-night drives with music cranked up and windows down. We remember the tears, the nights we drove alone through storms unsure if we would make it. I think of moments I have already shared, like sitting in the car outside a grocery store unable to remember why I had gone, realizing I had run myself down to fumes. Those moments, though painful, are part of the same rearview reflection. There were also nights I laughed so hard with my kids or a close friend that I forgot, even if just for a moment, how heavy life had been. Every memory becomes part of the mosaic of our lives. Each joy and each ache added color and shape to the person I am today.

Even the potholes and road closures served a purpose. They slowed me down when I thought I needed to rush. They rerouted me when I was too stubborn to change directions on my own. They forced me to pause, to reassess, to breathe. And the times I stalled, the jobs I lost, the relationships that ended, the seasons where nothing made sense, those were the moments that tested me the most. But looking back, they also taught me the most. They were not just interruptions, they were invitations to grow.

Looking in the rearview mirror also means acknowledging regret. I have taken some turns I should not have. I have stayed longer than I should have in situations that did not serve me. I have hurt people I loved by being too silent or too stubborn. And I have been hurt by people I thought would never leave. I have missed chances. I have let fear steer the wheel when faith should have been in charge. But rather than dwelling in shame, I choose to see those moments as part of the curriculum of life. Reflection gives us the opportunity to make peace with the past, to forgive ourselves and others, to let go, and to move forward lighter. Carrying bitterness only makes the drive harder. I have learned to unpack that weight and leave it behind.

Memory is also how we keep people with us. Those who have exited our lives through distance, circumstance, or death live on in our stories. My grandmother, my cousin, my godsister, they still ride with me in spirit. I feel their presence in quiet moments. I remember their laughter, their wisdom, their voice. I replay conversations I wish could have lasted longer. I visit memories like little keepsakes, knowing I cannot hold them physically but grateful I can return in my mind. The rearview mirror shows us they were real. They mattered. They helped shape who we are.

They shaped who I am. They shaped how I love, how I listen, how I forgive. And when the road gets hard, I find comfort in knowing they once sat beside me. Their presence, even if brief, helped me keep going. They may no longer be here physically, but they are part of every mile I travel.

For me, one of the memories that still makes me smile is when I think about how far I have come and the life I have created for myself, a life that my younger self could not have even imagined. I was the first in my family to travel to Asia, something that once felt like a distant, impossible dream. And now I get to let my children experience things that I only used to pray for. Watching them walk into possibilities that were never laid out for me is a joy that lives quietly in my heart. No announcement needed, just a sacred pride.

I still remember the moment it hit me. I was in Tokyo, standing with my sons on a quiet street, looking at the beautiful temples, and all I did was hug my boys and say, "Never be afraid to dream big." The air was humid and the sun was piercing through our skin, the faint scent of incense drifting from the temple grounds. Soft chanting from inside blended with the distant hum of city life. I could hear my boys laughing, their voices light against the stillness. The clean streets and minimal noises from the public transportation were so different from what we were accustomed to in New York City. In that moment, time felt suspended, and I wanted to memorize everything, from the sound of their slippers on the stone path to the way the sunlight caught their smiles. I glanced at them, tall, confident, curious, and felt tears sting my eyes. It was like witnessing a dream within a dream. That moment embodied the legacy I was shaping. The little girl who once clipped travel photos from magazines could have never predicted this. But here we were, walking a path she only dared to imagine.

Even more than that, I find myself deeply moved when I look at my parents and know I can help them in ways they once helped me. Seeing my mom no longer working as hard as she did over the years, and being able to support my dad in his later years, warms my heart. These moments may seem small from the outside, but to me, they are monumental. They are markers of growth, of healing, of the slow and steady transformation that time brings.

I have watched my parents carry so much through the years: responsibilities, burdens, sacrifices. They rarely complained. They just kept going. So now, being able to say, "I have got it," even in the smallest ways, feels like an honor. It feels like I am finally giving back to the people who gave me everything they could.

There is something deeply sacred about those slow exchanges, the unspoken gratitude between generations. I do not need them to say they are proud. I can feel it. And in those moments, I am proud too. Not just of the life I am building, but of the resilience it took to get here. These memories do not shout. They settle into the soul and remind me that the ride, with all its bumps and detours, was worth it. It reminds me of other moments from earlier miles, like when a friend offered a couch during a hard season or when a stranger's kindness redirected my route. The same quiet gratitude flows through all of them.

There was a time when I believed God had forgotten about me. Life had dealt me a difficult hand, and I often felt like my prayers were going unanswered. I expected divine intervention to come as thunder or light, as miracles I could point to and say, "That was God." But now, when I look back through the rearview mirror, I realize He was always there. He showed up in the kindness of strangers, in mentors who offered guidance, in friends who extended grace, and in the peaceful love that sustained me. It is one of the most important truths the road has taught me: God's presence is not always front and center, but it is always there. That regret, that ache of feeling abandoned, has softened into something else entirely. Gratitude.

Gratitude for the gentle ways He revealed Himself. For the strength I did not know I had. For the moments when I thought I was alone, only to later discover I was being carried. There was divine presence in the small gestures: a door held open, a phone call at the perfect time, a chance meeting that led to new direction. I began to understand that sometimes, miracles are not in your face. Sometimes, they come unannounced, glimmers you could miss if you're not looking. And sometimes that glimmer is all you need to keep going.

I carry the memory of my godsister most. Her battle with cancer was the first time I came face to face with death, not as an abstract idea but as something slow, heavy, and real. She died on my birthday. I still wrestle with that coincidence, unsure if it was meant to be a sign or a scar. What I do know is that it changed me. The last look in her eyes still visits me in quiet moments. I could not tell if she was afraid or at peace, but either way, her spirit stayed with me. She taught me to live and to fight.

There were nights I cried for her, and mornings I rose with her courage stitched into my chest like armor. Every year when my birthday comes, I remember her. Not in sadness, but in stillness. I light a candle or whisper a prayer. Her absence makes space for reflection. Her death made me confront the reality that we do not have forever, and that every mile counts. It takes me back to what I wrote earlier about the passengers who left the car too soon. They may have stepped out, but their influence keeps steering me in ways I could never repay.

She reminds me that while we are here, we must love hard, forgive quickly, and find joy in the little things. Because that is what she did. That is the legacy she left me: not just a memory, but a way of being. A way of riding this road with open eyes, a tender heart, and a fierce commitment to keep going.

There are other moments I wish I could go back to. I wish I had made it to my cousin's funeral. I wish I had been at my grandmother's bedside when she passed. She raised me, and not being there felt like a missed duty, like skipping the last chapter of a book that shaped me. I wish I had more time with my paternal grandfather and grandmother, and I wish I got to know my mother's father. These are not regrets I carry with guilt anymore, but with a tenderness that reminds me to be more present now, to cherish what and who I have while they are still in the car with me.

Time has a way of changing how we hold loss. When I was younger, I used to sit with those missed goodbyes and let them weigh on me like stones in my pockets. But now, I see those memories as gentle reminders to slow down, to reach out, to say what needs to be said before it is too late. I cannot rewrite those moments, but I can live differently because of them. I can show up more fully for the people I love. I can pause long enough to really listen, to hold a hand a few seconds longer, to be present even in the smallest ways.

Losing the chance to say goodbye does not mean the love was any less. If anything, it made the love more precious. It taught me that presence is not something we can put off. It is something we offer now, in real time, while the people we love are still riding beside us. And that awareness, though born from sorrow, has become a kind of wisdom I carry forward every day. It is the same wisdom that nudged me during earlier detours, the one that told me to stay in a conversation five minutes longer, or to turn around and say the thing I had been holding back.

The truth I have come to accept about my past is this: I have to keep moving. Because if I do not, life will push me in whichever direction the wind blows. I have learned that even when I feel stuck, forward is still an option. It might be slow. It might be quiet. It might look like simply getting out of bed or making one brave decision. But it is movement. And it is mine.

There was a season where everything around me felt uncertain. Once again, I left a job without a safety net waiting for me. My confidence was worn thin from trying to be everything for everyone. I felt suspended between who I had been and who I was becoming with no clear direction. That is when I learned the difference between drifting and driving. Drifting is passive. It is letting the world pull you along. But driving, even at five miles per hour, is an act of resistance. It is an act of faith.

I started to redefine what movement meant to me. It was not always big and bold. Sometimes it was putting my phone on silent so I could hear my own thoughts. Sometimes it was walking away from a toxic conversation, choosing peace over pleasing. Other times, it was saying yes to an opportunity even when fear whispered that I was not ready. Little by little, I started reclaiming my route. Just like in earlier chapters when I chose the harder road instead of the shortcut, these small moments reminded me that every turn is a choice.

And the beauty of forward motion is that it builds. One brave moment leads to another. A single step becomes a stride. Before you know it, you look up and realize you are no longer in the same place where you once felt stuck. That is the simple miracle of choosing to move, even when no one is watching.

Forward does not have to be flashy. It just has to be yours. And in claiming it, you reclaim your power. The road will not always be smooth, but as long as you are choosing your direction, you are still the one holding the wheel.

If I could speak to my younger self, the girl who questioned her worth, who bent herself to be accepted, who gave more than she had, I would tell her this, you were always enough. You did not have to earn love by shrinking yourself. You did not have to hustle for grace.

I would sit beside her, not to change her, but to remind her that her softness was not weakness, that her intuition was not foolishness, and that her voice, shaky and unsure, was still powerful. I would tell her that all the nights she cried alone, wondering if anyone saw her pain, were not wasted. They were moments of quiet becoming. She was growing in the dark, even when she could not see it.

I would tell her to stop apologizing for taking up space, for feeling too deeply, for dreaming too wildly. I would tell her that the road ahead would be hard, yes, filled with detours and disappointments, but every sharp turn would shape her. Every heartbreak would teach her how to rebuild. Every betrayal would help her find her own truth.

I would tell her to rest. To breathe. To stop trying to be perfect and instead just be real. That mess is beautiful. That healing is not linear. That joy does not have to be earned through suffering. I would remind her of the earlier roads we travelled, the times we survived on little more than hope and a half tank of courage, and how even then, we kept moving.

And when she asked me if it would all be worth it, I would look her in the eyes and say yes. Not because everything turns out how we plan, but because she will turn out to be someone strong, someone kind, someone honest, someone who, despite everything, still chooses hope. I would tell her that she is not alone. That the road, with all its twists and turns, is not a punishment, it is a passage. It is shaping her into a woman who knows where she is going and is proud, fiercely proud, of where she has been.

The rearview mirror reminds us that the journey has never been perfect, but it has always been ours. That realization does not erase the hard parts, but it honors them. Because everything behind us, even the broken pieces, played a role in building the person we have become.

Every detour held a lesson. Every delay forced us to slow down long enough to notice something we might have otherwise missed. The pain, the heartbreak, the silence, the nights we drove alone, those were not wasted. They shaped our courage. They refined our voice. They taught us how to keep going even when the road was unclear. They are the same lessons that carried me through earlier chapters of this journey, from the unexpected kindness of strangers to the detours that ended up saving me.

Looking back, I see not just the obstacles but the way I climbed over them. I see the strength I did not know I had. The forgiveness I gave when I could have stayed bitter. The dreams I kept alive even when everything around me told me to give up. The rearview mirror does not reflect perfection. It reflects truth. And the truth is, I have traveled far. Maybe not always fast. Maybe not always fearlessly. But faithfully. And that faith in myself, in God, in the journey, is what carried me through every mile.

And as we keep moving forward, we carry those reflections like quiet passengers. They ride with us in silence sometimes, whispering reminders in the spaces between songs or in the hush of the morning before the world wakes up. They shape how we drive, when to slow down, when to take the long way home, when to turn the music up and just breathe. They shift what we value, helping us recognize the beauty in simplicity, the strength in gentleness, the power in presence.

They change how we love. We learn to love more freely, less conditionally. We learn to say what matters, to hold hands a little longer, to forgive a little faster. The rearview does not tell us what is coming next, but it helps us reflect on where we have been. And somehow, that becomes its own kind of guidance, a compass that does not point north but inward, toward truth, toward healing, toward grace.

It is not about having the perfect route or knowing all the right turns. It is about recognizing the beauty in the path we have already walked. The one we etched ourselves, sometimes with trembling hands, sometimes with bold strokes. A path marked by laughter that echoed and grief that lingered. By doors we opened, and others we watched close. Every stretch of that road, every moment of silence, every whispered prayer, it all holds weight. It all holds worth.

And when we glance back with clarity, with kindness for the person we used to be, we gather strength for the journey ahead. We do not drive forward because we have all the answers, we drive forward because we finally understand the questions.

Because life's appointment with death is inevitable, but every mile before it is ours to shape, to savor, and to honor. That is what keeps me driving forward—not fear of the end, but love for the road I am still blessed to travel.

Arrival

Making Peace With the End of the Road

Eventually, every road trip ends. We pull into the final rest stop. Death is not a sudden detour; it is the destination we have been heading toward all along, but by the time we arrive, the hope is that we have lived in full color. We have loved. We have seen and done and felt. And if we have paid attention to the passengers and detours along the way, we can turn off the engine, take out the keys, and say, "I made the most of the ride."

Still, the idea of arriving can feel strange. After so much movement, so many twists and turns, so much searching and striving, what does it mean to stop? To rest? To be done? It is a thought that both comforts and unsettles us. But just like any road trip, when the final stretch comes into view, something inside us begins to shift. The urgency quiets. The noise softens. The memories start playing in our minds like a montage, each scene reminding us of earlier roads—the broken-down nights, the spontaneous scenic stops, the unexpected kindness of strangers, all the small proofs that we have been here, living. We see who we were when we started, who we became along the way, and who we are now, at the end.

I believe the end of the road can be gentle. Not a crash or a jolt, but a slowing down. A pull into familiar scenery. A breath. A knowing. By then, if we have lived honestly and loved well, there is nothing left to prove. There is only gratitude. Only rest. Only the quiet affirmation that we did not just exist, we truly lived. That is the gift of a full journey. Not perfection, not the absence of pain, but the presence of meaning. A life marked by moments that mattered. A road trip that left its mark not just on the map, but on the hearts of those we traveled with.

The end of the journey can feel daunting, mysterious, even fearful. But it can also be peaceful, a sense of arriving where we were always meant to go. Just as a road trip comes to a close with familiar landmarks fading into the distance and the hum of the engine quieting, so too does life gradually lead us toward rest. Not an end, but a transition. A surrender. A serene acceptance that we are no longer striving, climbing, or pushing forward, but instead settling into the grace of stillness. It is the moment when the noise fades, the striving softens, and we let go not because we have given up, but because we have finally arrived.

And when that moment comes, perhaps we will remember how many times the road taught us this same truth before—in grief, in letting go of seasons, in the bittersweet goodbyes to earlier passengers—that arrival is not loss, it is transformation.

Where we once saw death as a thief, we can begin to see it instead as a gentle usher guiding us to a place beyond exhaustion, beyond worry. For those who have carried much, fought hard, and loved deeply, there is something sacred about knowing that rest is near. It is the place where the story hands itself over to something greater, just as every ending along the way once opened into a new beginning.

I remember standing at my godsister's funeral, a day when the air felt heavy and the scent of fall filled the air and the look and the faces of everyone, her passing forever etched into my soul because it happened on my birthday. I stood there, surrounded by flowers, muffled sobs, and the low hum of whispered condolences, trying to make sense of life and death in the same breath. It was the first time I looked mortality in the face and realized that it was not just a philosophical concept or something reserved for old age. Death had a name, a face, a story: hers.

We weren't close, but in the end she felt close. Watching her fade away from cancer was like watching a light dim slowly, painfully, until it was gone. Her strength amazed me, even in her suffering. The way she held on to small joys, even as her body failed her, was something I will never forget. But nothing could prepare me for the void she left behind. That void felt even bigger because it landed on a day that was always meant for celebration. In the years afterward, birthdays were a sad time for me. They reminded me that the day I was given life is also the day I experienced someone losing theirs.

And in the strange way life works, her death gave birth to a deeper awareness in me, that life, every breath of it, was precious, unpredictable, and temporary. I began to see each day not as something owed to me, but as something gifted. I learned to cherish the ordinary, the way sunlight spills through a window, the sound of my children laughing, the quiet moments of stillness that remind me I am alive. Her absence became one of my greatest teachers, shaping how I now greet both mornings and goodbyes. Her final breath taught me to breathe with more intention.

To this day, I carry her with me. Not just in memory, but in the way I live. She reminds me to fight through the hard days and find joy in the easy ones. She reminds me that every mile matters, even the painful ones. And she reminds me that death, while inevitable, is also the reason we must live fully, love deeply, and never take a single sunrise for granted.

There was a stillness that followed her passing, a kind of quiet I had not known before. And in that silence, I started asking myself: What does it mean to really live? What legacy will I leave? What will the last mile of my journey say about how I traveled?

It was not just the absence of her voice or laughter that made the world feel quieter. It was the realization that life does not wait. That it moves forward whether we are ready or not. The day she passed, I wasn't in any mood to celebrate. I had just received the heartbreaking news that my kids' aunt in Paris was dying from cancer, and I was making arrangements to fly there the following day. Earlier that morning, my godfather had called me to tell me my godsister wasn't doing well and asked if I wanted to visit. I told him no. Later, around 5 or 6 p.m., the phone rang again and this time he simply said, "She just went home."

When I arrived in Paris and saw my kids' aunt, the reality struck even harder. Cancer had aged her so much. Even her dog was dying of cancer, as if he were trying to stay by her side beyond the end. My first night in that house was heartbreaking. It was the weight of an unfinished life I couldn't understand. Shopping bags she had filled months earlier were still sitting there with the tags on. Her son's father had taken him, and the half-built Lego set he'd left behind remained untouched. It was the most unfinished life I have ever witnessed.

I remember waking up on my birthday, the day she died, and everything felt different. The celebration felt hollow, the cake untouched, and the phone calls awkward. That year, my birth and her death shared the same date and I could no longer separate beginnings from endings.

At the final stretch, we begin to review the entire map. We look back at the beginnings, the detours, the passengers, the pit stops, the breakdowns, the victories, and the scenic views. We see how it all connected. How the rough roads led to resilience. How every earlier detour, even the ones I once resented, delivered me to a place I could not have reached any other way. I think about the days I struggled, the nights I questioned my worth, and the seasons I nearly gave up. And then I think about where I am now, how every stumble taught me something, how every loss deepened my capacity to love.

We start to see death not as a thief, but as a witness to all the living we have done. It watches silently as we laugh, fall in love, raise children, make mistakes, and build something out of nothing. It does not interrupt us, but it waits. And when it finally arrives, it does not come to erase us. It comes to remind us that we were here. That we lived. That we made something beautiful with the time we were given.

And when I think of those who arrived at the destination before me—my godsister, my cousin, my grandmothers, my grandfathers, and even the friends who were once constant voices in my life but drifted away—I feel their presence still riding with me. Their love lingers in the soft moments, like when I hear a certain song, or when the wind brushes across my face in just the right way. I do not feel far from them. They are like headlights in the rearview mirror, faint but steady, lighting the way forward. They simultaneously feel like mile markers I passed a while back, reminding me I am getting closer.

Sometimes, it is a scent that catches me off guard, like the hair oil my grandmother used, or the contagious smile of my cousin with his white teeth and jet-black gum. Other times, it is a phrase, a look in my sons' eyes, or even a moment of quiet when I can almost hear their laughter. It is in these brief flashes that I am reminded that love does not die, it simply changes its seat in the car. These small, almost invisible afterimages carry so much weight. They are the sacred reminders that although their journeys ended before mine, their impact did not. They helped shape my roadmap.

I carry them in my heart like treasured passengers I had to drop off but never truly let go of. I remember their stories, their struggles, their grace, and I let their memory teach me how to keep going, how to love deeper, speak kinder, and hold on to joy even in sorrow. They are not gone. They are ahead of me, waiting at the final stop. And until then, I drive on, guided by the legacy they left behind and the quiet comfort that one day, I will see them again.

Sometimes, late at night, I wonder about my own final mile. What will it look like? Will I have said what mattered? Loved the way I wanted to? Forgiven fully? There is no real answer to that question except this: I am trying. Every day, I am trying.

Trying to speak with honesty, even when my voice trembles. Trying to love the people in my life with more presence, not just intention. Trying to forgive myself for the things I did not know then and to extend that same grace to others. Trying to show up for my children in ways I wish someone had shown up for me. Trying to savor the mornings I used to rush through, the faces I used to take for granted, the breath I used to ignore. Trying, above all, to keep the tank full enough for one more mile, one more act of kindness, one more laugh.

Some nights, the wondering feels heavier. I ask if my story will echo after I am gone, if anything I have done will matter to those I leave behind. But even in that uncertainty, I find peace in the effort. Because this life, this messy, beautiful, aching, breathtaking life, was never meant to be perfected. It was meant to be lived. Fully. Bravely. And with love.

So I keep trying. And maybe that is what the final mile is about. Not having everything figured out, but knowing that you walked the road as best you could, with your heart open and your eyes wide. That you kept going, even when the path was not clear. That you tried, and tried again, until the very end.

So when the moment comes, when I park the car, take one last look through the windshield, and prepare to exit, may it be with a gentle smile. Not because the road was easy, but because it was mine. I showed up. I risked. I loved. I grew. I grieved. I celebrated. I gave, and I received. And every curve and crack in that road carries my fingerprints, proof that I did not just pass through, I was here.

And in that final pause, I hope to feel a quiet knowing settle over me, a peace that whispers, "You did what you came to do. Not everything, not perfectly, but purposefully." I hope to see flashes of the lives I touched, the laughter I shared, the tears I helped dry. I hope the ones I love know they were cherished. I hope my children carry the strength I tried to live by and the softness I learned to embrace along the way.

I want to meet the end not with fear, but with grace. Not clinging to what I wish I had done differently, but grateful for what I did. The detours, the delays, the scenic routes I never expected, they were all part of the ride. I did not just make it to the destination. I lived the miles.

Death is not a detour; it is the arrival point of the journey. But how we reach it matters. The destination is certain, but the quality of the ride is not. If I have learned anything from the roads I have already traveled, from the breakdowns that forced me to pause, from the sunsets I almost missed, from the passengers who shaped me, it is that living fully is the best preparation for the end. When we live fully, love deeply, and reflect often, we can meet our final stop with peace.

The engine turns off, but the path traveled remains. And somewhere beyond the horizon, perhaps, a new road begins.

I remember a moment that made me think about this truth in a deeper way. It was years ago, during a late summer evening, and I was sitting on my front steps, watching the sun dip below the skyline. There had been a funeral that day, a distant relative, someone I had not been particularly close to, but whose death still managed to stir something in me. Maybe it was the look in their children's eyes, or the weight of unspoken things that hung in the air.

As I sat there in the soft golden quiet, I thought about how fragile everything is. How quickly life turns. The sound of cicadas hummed in the background, and the air smelled faintly of cut grass and warm asphalt, like the end of summer itself was saying goodbye. I promised myself that I did not want to be someone who merely existed. I wanted to leave fingerprints on the hearts of others. I wanted to be remembered not for perfection, but for presence, for showing up, for loving deeply, for creating moments that mattered.

It was a simple moment, but it changed something in me. It made me aware that how I travel, how I show up on this road, will determine how I arrive. And when that moment comes, when I pull into the final rest stop, I want to do so with no gas left in the tank. I want to know I used it all, every ounce of love, every laugh, every lesson, every scar.

Because if death is the end of this road, then I want the journey to have been worth it. Not just for me, but for everyone who rode with me along the way.

If I am remembered for anything, let it be that I did not just drive fast or far, but that I paid attention to the road, to the passengers, to the lessons. That I made meaning out of the miles. That I welcomed each stop, each turn, each goodbye with open eyes and a willing heart.

Let it be said that I did not just race toward the end, but that I paused often enough to feel the sun on my skin, to laugh at roadside diners, to cry at rest stops, and to sit in silence when the view called for reverence. I want to be remembered as someone who did not waste the ride, who did not wait for perfect weather or perfect company to enjoy the drive.

May they say I paid attention to people. That I did not overlook the quiet ones in the back seat or take for granted the ones who shared the wheel when I was too tired to steer. That I listened, truly listened, and made room for others to feel seen, heard, and valued. May they remember that when storms came, I kept the wipers moving, kept the music playing, and kept hope in the glove compartment, just in case someone else needed it too.

And if the map of my life is ever studied, I hope the lines are messy but meaningful. Full of side streets taken out of curiosity, of loops made for love, of dead ends that taught me patience, and scenic routes that reminded me to slow down.

I want my children to say, "She made every mile count. Not by getting there first, but by making sure we saw everything worth seeing along the way." I want those who knew me to feel that I lived with both hands on the wheel and my heart wide open. That I drove with courage, navigated with hope, and carried grace in the glove compartment for when the road got rough.

That, more than anything, would be enough. Because in the end, the journey was never just about the destination. It was about how I drove, who I became, and the love I left behind. It was about how I turned breakdowns into lessons, detours into discoveries, and passengers into family. It was about the quiet mornings when I chose to rise despite the weight of yesterday. The hard conversations I did not avoid. The dreams I chased even when they scared me. The apologies I offered, the forgiveness I extended. The lessons I finally learned after getting lost, circling back, and starting again. The truth is, I did not always know where I was headed, but I chose to keep going anyway. That is what mattered.

I think of the people I met along the way, some who stayed, some who left, and some who simply passed through long enough to teach me something I did not know I needed. Each of them added something to my road, whether it was laughter that lightened the ride or pain that sharpened my direction. I remember moments of joy that felt like sun warming my arm through the window, and moments of sorrow that poured like rain on the windshield, blurring my view but never stopping my movement.

If I am remembered for anything, let it be that I did not just drive fast or far, but that I paid attention. That I noticed the trees lining the road, the faces in the rearview, the changing seasons in my spirit. That I did not speed past my life but slowed down enough to savor it. That I let people in. That I made space. That I made meaning.

I hope I am remembered not for how perfectly I navigated the route, but for how deeply I loved during the ride. I hope the people I touched along the way felt seen, heard, and held. I hope they know that even when I made wrong turns, I still carried them with care. I hope they remember how I showed up, even when I was scared. How I kept my heart soft even when life tried to harden it. How I did not run from the storms, but learned to drive through them, wipers on, heart wide open.

And when that last mile comes, when I pull into the final stop and turn off the ignition, I want it to be with peace in my chest and gratitude in my soul. No regrets for roads I did not take, just awe for the ones I did. I want to look out the windshield one last time and smile, knowing that I lived a life that meant something. That I did not just pass through, but that I paved something behind me.

Let it be said, "She took the long way when it mattered, the shortcuts when she had to, and the scenic route whenever she could. She gave directions to those who needed them and never hesitated to stop for someone stranded. She rode with courage. She broke down and got back up. She filled her tank with hope, even on empty roads."

Because in the end, it was never just about the destination. It was about shaping the miles before it arrived. Life's appointment with death is inevitable, but every moment before it is ours to claim, to color, and to make unforgettable. The engine quiets. The sky opens. And somewhere just beyond the horizon, the next road waits, ready for the final chapter of this journey.

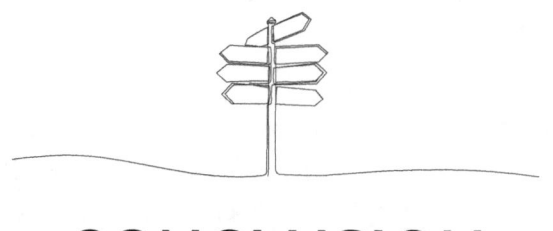

CONCLUSION

You're Still Driving: Choose How You'll Travel From Here

So, as you sit behind the wheel each day, remember you're not just driving aimlessly. You're heading somewhere. But don't be in a rush. Roll down the windows. Let the wind hit your face. Laugh with your passengers. Cry when you need to. Pull over sometimes. Take the scenic route.

Because every mile matters. And though we're all headed to the same appointment, it's how we travel that defines the journey. Make it count. Life is not a race to the end, but a sacred ride between two points. It's meant to be experienced with intention, not urgency. We're here to engage with the world, to see it, feel it, taste it, love it. We're here to gather stories, not just miles. To build connections, not just accomplishments.

When you pause to notice the little things, the way sunlight spills across the dashboard, the sound of laughter echoing from the back seat, the simple joy of finding the perfect song for the moment, you're not wasting time. You're honoring it.

Yes, there will be moments of frustration. Detours you didn't plan. Breakdowns you didn't foresee. But there will also be stargazing on the hood of the car, and spontaneous dance parties at gas stations. There will be silence that comforts and conversations that heal. These are the pieces that make the journey yours. You won't always know where the next turn leads. That's okay. The road was never meant to be entirely predictable. What matters is that you show up, heart open, eyes wide, and you drive.

And as you drive, remember the passengers you've picked up and let go of along the way, the ones whose laughter still lingers, the ones whose wisdom still guides you, and even the ones whose absence taught you what presence really means. Remember the detours that felt like delays but turned out to be blessings. Recall the moments you thought were wrong turns, only to discover they were leading you exactly where you needed to go. These memories are your mile markers, proof that you've been moving, learning, and becoming.

May your tank be full. May your passengers be kind. May your path unfold with grace. And when you finally reach your destination, may you be able to say: I didn't just arrive. I truly lived.

Now, go enjoy the ride. But before you go, let me tell you what this journey has meant to me. Writing this book was never just about telling a story. It was about finding the courage to share mine. To look back on the roads I've taken, the potholes I hit, the passengers I lost, the quiet victories I never celebrated aloud, and say, "Here it is. This was my ride."

There were days I didn't think I'd make it. Days I felt lost, overlooked, or broken beyond repair. But somehow, grace found me. Through every wrong turn, every reroute, every moment I wanted to give up, I kept driving.

This book became my rearview mirror. It helped me see how far I've come, how much I've grown, and how deeply I still believe in love, resilience, and redemption. I am not the same person I was when I began writing this. I am braver. Softer. Wiser. And more committed than ever to living a life that is real. I think about the "passengers" you've met in these pages, my godsister, my grandmother, my cousin, my children, my parents, and how each one shaped the way I drive. I think about the long nights, the quiet sunrises, the unexpected conversations that changed my route forever. If my story has touched you in any way, it's because their fingerprints are all over it. This isn't just my ride. It's ours.

To you, the reader, the traveler beside me, thank you. Thank you for riding along, for listening to my stories, and for seeing pieces of your own reflection in these pages. I hope something here reminds you that your journey matters too. That your voice belongs. That your path, no matter how winding, has worth.

If you remember anything from this book, let it be this: life's appointment with death is unavoidable, but every mile before it is yours to shape, to savor, and to claim as your own. You are still driving. You get to choose how you travel from here.

Take your time. Find your rhythm. Create meaning.

And above all, don't just pass through life.

Live it.

I like to imagine us now, you and I, parked for a moment at some scenic overlook. Maybe we're sipping coffee, maybe the car radio hums softly in the background. The road behind us is full of stories, the road ahead full of mystery. You'll drive on from here, and I'll drive on from here too, but for a brief moment, we've shared the same stretch of highway. That, to me, is a gift.

I'll be somewhere down the road, cheering you on.

ABOUT THE AUTHOR

Venice Ishibashi is a storyteller, a mother, and a lifelong seeker of meaning along life's winding roads. Born in Jamaica and raised in New York, her journey has been shaped by both chosen paths and unexpected turns, each leaving her with lessons, resilience, and stories worth sharing.

She earned an Associate Degree in Liberal Arts and a Bachelor's Degree in Psychology with a minor in criminal justice, both from Medgar Evers College, graduating with honors. She later went on to earn a Master of Science in Instructional Design and Technology from Western Illinois University, an experience that not only deepened her knowledge but also strengthened her passion for understanding life, embracing differences, and empowering others.

Over the years, Venice's work in higher education and community building has been fueled by a single driving force: to help others discover their voice, their courage, and their direction.

When she's not writing or leading, Venice enjoys listening to country music, exploring New York City, and playing with fashion, activities that keep her grounded and inspired. She is also the proud mother of two sons who serve as her compass and her greatest motivation, reminding her daily to love fiercely, show up fully, and keep moving forward even when the road ahead is unclear.

Driving to My Appointment With Death is her debut book—a heartfelt reflection on living with intention, loving deeply, and embracing every mile, even the ones we never saw coming. Venice is still driving, still learning, and still showing up with an open heart, hands on the wheel, and eyes on the horizon.

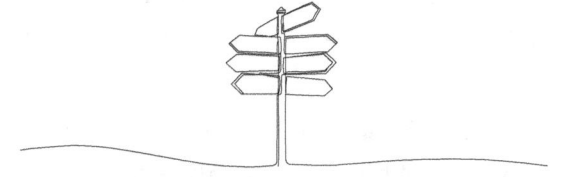

ACKNOWLEDGEMENTS

The journey of writing this book has been both deeply personal and profoundly transformational. While my name is on the cover, this work stands on the shoulders of so many. I am grateful beyond words to every person who walked, rode, prayed, and cheered me through this road.

First, I give thanks to God for entrusting me with this message, for lighting the way in dark tunnels, and for giving me the strength to keep driving when the road felt endless. Your grace has been my compass and my rest stop.

To my children, Zachary and Josh Ishibashi, thank you for being the truest passengers on this road. Your love, your strength, and your laughter gave this journey meaning. Everything I've done, I've done with you in my heart.

To my parents, Joyce Robinson and Linval Edwards, thank you for the sacrifices, the prayers, and the foundation you built for me. I carry your lessons with me every mile I travel.

To my godsister, cousin, grandparents, and all the loved ones who arrived at their final destination before me, your lives continue to shape my steps. I write with you in mind and carry you in spirit.

To my Godfather, Papa, thank you for your support in writing about my experience. Special thanks to the Roseau Ladies for cheering me on during this journey.

To my extended family, thank you for showing up for me in ways that words can never fully capture. To Nadine Edwards, your encouragement and belief in me gave me courage in moments of doubt. Thanks to Theresa Nicholson, Lakeisha Davis, and Ricardo Edwards for your love and support.

To the friends who became family—Christian Ishibashi, Arlene Williams, and Wainright Elbers and family—thank you for standing by me in the hard moments and celebrating the beautiful ones. Your presence helped me stay the course.

To my mentors and guides—Denene Rodney and Dr. Evelyn Castro—your wisdom, encouragement, and honest feedback shaped both this book and the writer I am becoming. Thank you for challenging me to go deeper and be braver.

To my self-publishing expert and writing coach, Reea Rodney, thank you for challenging me to go deeper, to be braver, and to show up fully. This wouldn't be what it is without your wisdom and encouragement.

To the incredible professionals at Dara Publishing, thank you for bringing this book to life with such care and excellence. You not only created a design that beautifully reflects my vision, your dedication and skill made this journey less daunting and more joyful. I am grateful for your expertise, your patience, and your belief in this project.

To every person who shared their story with me, thank you for your vulnerability and trust. Your voices echo in these pages.

To every reader who picked up this book, thank you for giving me your time, your attention, and your trust. I hope you saw yourself here. I hope you felt less alone. And I hope you're reminded that your journey matters.

With love and gratitude, I leave you with this prayer: that God will guide your road ahead, light your path in dark moments, and fill your journey with grace.

With love and gratitude,
Venice

THANK YOU!

Thank you for taking the time to journey with me through *Driving to My Appointment With Death*. Writing this book was both healing and humbling, and it means so much that you chose to share in these reflections. My hope is that the stories and lessons within these pages offered you moments of clarity, comfort, and connection.

If this book touched your heart, encouraged you, or gave you something meaningful to reflect on, I would be deeply grateful if you could take a few minutes to leave a review on Amazon. Your feedback not only supports my work as an author but also helps other readers discover this book and find encouragement for their own journeys.

With gratitude,
Venice Ishibashi